Yes, Sir! No, Sir!
No Excuse, Sir!
"Finding Lost Honor"

ROBERT GEORGE

WESTBOW
PRESS®
A DIVISION OF THOMAS NELSON
& ZONDERVAN

WestBow Press books may be ordered through booksellers or by contacting:

WestBow Press
A Division of Thomas Nelson & Zondervan
1663 Liberty Drive
Bloomington, IN 47403
www.westbowpress.com
1 (866) 928-1240

ISBN: 978-1-5127-6197-9 (sc)
ISBN: 978-1-5127-6198-6 (hc)
ISBN: 978-1-5127-6196-2 (e)

Library of Congress Control Number: 2016917658

Print information available on the last page.

WestBow Press rev. date: 10/31/2016

To Judy George, beautiful in body, soul, and spirit. Thanks for taking the risk and sharing our journey of faith. I love you wholeheartedly!

To Sandra and Michael, who, along with their spouses, Wes and Carolyn, have at times tolerated but more often loved me, and blessed me with four amazing grandchildren:

Clarissa, USNA '16, America's newest ensign who carries the patriotic torch! Go, girl!

Jacob, a bright college graduate with a warrior's heart, and my favorite grandson!

Madeline, beauty, brains, talent, and the spirit to conquer mountains on a bike!

Marjorie, beautiful, bright, talented beyond measure, and poetry on horseback!

To my sisters Trish and Sharon, who shared my journey and still love me.

To Bob Ritter, '67, who took me fishing and hooked me.

To Greg and Kathy who nurtured me.

To all who wear "The Ring," especially my brothers from Romeo '67.

To The Citadel, an institution that has maintained its core value of honor. Go, Dogs!

To 58,307 American heroes whose names are engraved on a black granite wall in Washington, DC. Their dreams ended prematurely, but their honor continues.

Contents

PREFACE

Throughout my childhood, I learned to deflect blame and offer excuses for offenses both real or imagined. By doing so, I avoided the need to examine my own heart and to make the changes needed for a healthy and mature life. In short, I dragged immature emotional responses into my adult life and watched them sabotage my marriage and careers. Life's challenging events often brought outbursts of jealousy, anger and blame, and such outbursts wounded me and those around me. I lacked the ability to cope maturely with the pain of friends lost in war and dreams lost to the pressures of life. Without mature faith, I found myself disillusioned and adrift.

My parents tried to modify my behavior from an early age with punishments ranging from timeouts, writing "I will not ..." five hundred times, standing in front of the mirror for a period of time, mouth washings with Ivory soap, forced apologies, and spankings. I heard Mom say a few hundred times, "Bobby George, I love you, and this is going to hurt me more than you, but I'm going to spank the devil out of you." Only five foot one and a hundred pounds wet, she wielded a stinging, eighteen-inch sewing ruler with the expertise of a marine drill instructor. Eventually my bottom took on the consistency of brown leather oxfords, and I grew to like the taste of Ivory soap, but somewhere the devil hung on and grinned.

Lest you think I was a horrid kid, let me assure you that I blended well with my peers. I usually sought the middle ground so as not to draw undue attention. I was a ready follower but seldom led others in bad behavior. Attendance at Sunday school failed to make me a "good boy," although I fooled some. At age seven, I was chosen as the groom for a

"Tom Thumb" wedding at church. That occasioned wearing my first tux and my first kiss with the bride. Ugh … girls! Cooties!

I learned to deflect blame at an early age, as a yellowed typewritten note to my mother demonstrates. She had kept it among her "treasures" and it passed on to me after her death (typos included):

Dear Mother,   April 18, 1957
    I like you very much. IAlso think that you are a very good cook.
    So wwould you please cook a roasted turkey. For I love turkey espically roast turkey.
    Ialso t hink you and daddy are good parents. But sometimes you get mad and we don't like it, but it is our own fault.
    I am going to try to be better but I can't if the girls keep doing things. But I will try my best.
    Love Bobby.

By age eleven, I was honing the art of flattery and blame. (Sorry, my sweet sisters.) Did you notice that the note began with "I," changed to "we," and finally to "our"? The only individual I omitted was the devil! (Apologies to comedian Flip Wilson and Geraldine.) I can't say if Mom served roasted turkey that April, but I'm certain that I continued to blame others for my misdeeds and failures long after this was written. In fact, I learned to wield sarcasm with the expertise of an Olympic fencer. By deflecting attention and blame to others, I avoided the need to examine my own heart, or so I thought.

Join me on this journey as I share some epic failures and painful lessons learned on the road to becoming the man God always desired. A man after God's own heart.

Let's start at Ground Zero.

PROLOGUE

In early December 2001, I left the rest center at Ground Zero seeking fresh air and a brief respite from the unrelenting sights, sounds, smells, and grief emanating from the horrific pit where great towers once stood. The dank church cellar was a place of refuge for exhausted first responders continuing the gruesome recovery effort now in its second month. I tightened my jacket collar and pulled my cap lower as the brisk winter wind bit at my face and ears. Passing Wall Street's great brass bull statue, a few snowflakes danced teasingly on the wind. I walked aimlessly, eventually finding myself near the old docks and ancient commercial buildings that comprised the nascent city along the East River. Here strong arms and backs had first hauled a young nation's merchandise and trade. Could the early settlers of colonial America have possibly dreamed that such a great city would emerge from their meager beginnings or be so grievously wounded by evil? I walked on, enjoying the relative solitude of empty streets and the freshening air while thanking God for the opportunity to serve Him at Ground Zero.

Turning a corner, I walked toward a crowd encircling the front entrance to a fire station. I noticed a growing memorial to the 343 FDNY casualties at Ground Zero comprised of flowers, pictures, notes, candles, and other items of remembrance as the public attempted to thank its firefighters and share in their collective grief. Photoflashes lit the scene, illuminating a firefighter's tired face staring blankly from within. Exhausted from long weeks of difficult physical and emotional duty, the firefighters sat imprisoned by the crowd.

As I continued past, a firefighter opened the side door away from the public. I waved and continued walking.

He shouted, "Are you looking for T-shirts like everyone else?" (Some fire companies were selling T-shirts to raise funds for the families of fallen firefighters.)

I hesitated and replied, "No, I'm just a tired fire chaplain taking a walk."

He continued insistently, "Really, a fire chaplain? Come in. Hurry before they see you."

The metal door slammed with finality behind me.

He asked, "Father, did they send you from downtown?" When I replied that I lived in Orange County, he sighed and said, "Father, there's someone you need to talk with now. Come on!"

He left me no time to explain that I wasn't a priest and that my Orange County was in California, not New York.

We walked through the apparatus room where a normally spotless truck and engine sat forlornly covered with the smell and detritus of service at Ground Zero. Several other firefighters hurriedly avoided our approach. I followed into the dated watch office where an exhausted firefighter sat doubled over, deeply sobbing into his hands. Without further words, the first firefighter quickly left the room.

Reaching deeply for each breath, his body heaved from effort, but there was no acknowledgment of my presence from the sobbing firefighter. The depth of his distress reminded me of the dark night many years before, when my own life had disintegrated. I sat near him in the small office and silently prayed. It was perhaps ten minutes before he acknowledged me with red, swollen eyes and runny nose. In the coming hour, a torrent of grief and anger engulfed me as he choked out his painful story. This firehouse had lost twelve men from the engine and truck companies during the Tower's collapse. All had been close friends. He had attended their funerals in the weeks following the attack along with those of his brother, an uncle, and a number of friends also lost at Ground Zero. He was battling survivor's guilt and post-traumatic stress magnified by physical exhaustion. Working almost continuously since September 11, he said that he had almost forgotten what his wife and children looked like. On a recent day off, he and his wife had fought. She wanted her husband back, but he had lost himself in the days and weeks following September 11. He had little left to give, and she was unwilling to settle for what remained. They had parted with angry threats of divorce and had not spoken since that day. Just moments before I entered the station, he had received a phone call that his father had been rushed to a hospital with cardiac failure. His company officer had refused his request to leave the station to be with him and required him to remain on duty until a replacement could be found. There was nearly a physical altercation before cooler heads separated the two. He sat before me broken in every aspect and cried aloud, seeking an end to the pain. The juggernaut of grief overwhelmed me, and I desperately grasped for a shred of wisdom from my critical care training. I slid the chair closer until our knees touched, and taking his hand, I asked if I could pray for him. He simply nodded. I have no remembrance of the words spoken. They were not grandly spiritual, but I know that God heard and joined two men in a moment of shared grief. Tears glistened on our cheeks as I softly interceded for healing in his life and marriage, for his father's healing, and for his strength to carry on. After sitting quietly for several minutes, he arose and crushed me in a bear hug. He sighed and, in a thick New York accent, quietly said, "Father, you are a gift from God. You just saved my life. I'll never forget you. You are my angel." I offered to stay longer, but he declined, saying he needed to ready himself for duty. Slipping out the side door, I turned toward Ground Zero with thoughts soaring about a God who would send a fire chaplain three thousand miles to meet a firefighter in the deep pit of personal crisis. I realized that my walk hadn't been aimless and that God had purposed every step. Humming a praise song, I thanked Him for the privilege of serving Him. I pondered competing thoughts of exhaustion and exhilaration while realizing that God was overcoming evil through many such acts of small graces. He was willing to use all who heard His call and responded, even me.

Yet, it wasn't always so. For over a decade, I had run from God, not to Him. I allowed the world and the hypocrisy I found in church to extinguish the spiritual training of my early childhood. Along the way, there were bitter lessons learned and painful experiences that have made me, by God's redemption, who I am, scars and all. My story isn't one of child abuse, great fame, or substance addiction but the dissolution of shattered expectations and dreams that caused me to lose my moral compass and my honor and to doubt my faith. It also caused me to lose hope in the American dream. For thirty-three years, I allowed the noise of life to drown out the still, small voice of God.

I have included stories to give context and color to the seasons of my life, but I have intentionally avoided overtly graphic, gratuitous, or salacious accounts of behavior and violence. The stories and conversations herein are my best recollections, and names have been changed where privacy is appropriate.

I hope both my failures and lessons learned will resonate with you as you face your own challenging life journey and discover God's calling for your life.

Let's begin in Clearwater, Florida, in 1989.

BEGINNINGS

The day following my father's memorial service, I sat alone on the windowed porch of my parents' Florida house where they had retired from Baltimore ten years before. I sat engulfed by the flood of thoughts and emotions issuing from a seemingly bottomless well of grief. I missed Dad, and the realization that I would never again hold him or speak to him overwhelmed my senses. I reflected how poorly I had spoken at his service, being overcome by raw emotions. I criticized myself for both my lack of eloquence and guilt for not having been with him when he died. Distance and the cost of airline tickets had once seemed rational excuses, but they now seemed selfish, petty reasons for not having been there for him. I understood the biblical truths of Dad's salvation, but today I grieved.

I reflected on our last time together following his cancer diagnosis. Just a year before, he and I had driven to the supermarket but sat imprisoned in the car by a sudden thunderstorm. Judy had prayerfully encouraged me to make the trip to settle my heart about his faith and impending death. During the rainstorm, the spirit of God moved.

"Dad, you know I gave my heart to Christ in 1979, and it has changed my life dramatically. According to scripture, I have eternal life through Christ and will dwell in the presence of God. I want to know that you'll be there to greet me when I arrive. Dad, you've always been a good man, but have you accepted Christ as your Lord and Savior?"

"I'm not sure," he replied.

"Would you like to pray and accept Christ now?" Those words brought the image of a small fishing boat in Biscayne Bay back into focus.

"Yes, I think I would like to pray."

We shared a prayer of confession and faith in Jesus Christ, and the rain abruptly stopped. That day, a father and son became brothers in Christ. A few days later, I flew back to California. It would be our last time together in this life.

My sisters, Patricia and Sharon, sat with Mom in the living room, quietly knitting and reading. As time and geography separated our family over the years, the priorities of marriages and careers had taken precedence. Family ties had unraveled into occasional phone calls, greeting cards, and infrequent visits. Trish entered the kitchen where the clattering dishes meant she would soon be busy making our lunch. I selfishly hoped it wouldn't be leftover ham for the third meal in a row since Dad's memorial service.

By any measure, Grafton Lee George was a good man. Born in 1911, he had lost his father at age six. His mother, unable to support two young children, received a scholarship for Dad to attend McDonough Military School for Orphaned Boys outside of Baltimore. His younger brother, Joseph, remained with his mother. Dad lived at McDonough from elementary through high school. The military training stood him in good stead when he was drafted into the army in World War II. Between 1942 and 1945, Dad was promoted from private to captain in the army serving at the Pentagon. During his childhood, he saw the development of both airplanes and automobiles. Before his death, he saw man step on the moon in America's bold venture into outer space.

Following the war, he loved and cared for his family through many lean, hard years working for the Western Maryland Railroad. Postwar years saw low wages and many furloughs. Dad often worked second jobs to provide for us. He worked night shifts and weekends and was routinely sleep deprived, yet he seldom showed worry or raised his hand in anger. Dad was a gentleman in the best meaning of that term. On several occasions while I was in elementary school and junior high, he took me to work the night shift with him at the railroad. I would spend the shift on a switch engine with a trusted engineer, and the love of trains was born. Many of my buddies had Lionels, but I had real trains and my dad's excuse from school!

Mom, all five feet one inch, wore the chevrons of sergeant of arms and administered family discipline, along with copious amounts of love and laughter. I found that when I could deflect Mom's well-deserved corporal punishments long enough by chases around the dining room table or backyard, she would start laughing, and sometimes the punishment would be forgiven as we dissolved into hugs and tickles.

Mom was a woman of faith, and I knew she understood the truth of eternal life and salvation in Jesus Christ, but at times of loss, theological truths are often better unspoken, as the grieving heart needs rest and space to recover from shock. And so we sat apart, each nursing our grief and seeking rest, in the cold aftermath of death. Trish had cared for Dad many times during the year he battled cancer. She had nursed him tenderly, and I believe his death hit her the hardest of the three siblings. When she called us into the kitchen for lunch, the ham sandwiches she served caused me to criticize her, as my selfishness trumped empathy for her emotional needs. My critical comments added to the pain of Mom's broken heart.

Following a tense lunch, I retreated back to the porch and attempted to lose myself in the voluminous military files Dad had kept over the years. Mom had asked me to see if any should be kept and to dispose of the rest. Dad had maintained detailed copies of his army records from induction as a private until his retirement years later as a major in the army reserve. On autopilot, I discarded paper after paper and was about to add yet another to the trash when I hesitated. I reexamined the yellowed weekend leave form giving him permission to return home to Baltimore and smiled. Entering the living room, I asked, "Mom, do you remember this weekend leave with Dad in early February 1945?"

Looking quizzical, she replied, "No, why should I?"

Smiling, I asked, "Mom, what happened nine months from that weekend?"

She looked at the form again, and with the hint of a smile, she replied, "Oh my, I guess I should have remembered that weekend!"

The smile broadened and illumined her face for the first time since Dad's death as she was taken back to a brief weekend of loving intimacy with the man who had been her faithful husband for forty-eight years.

3

My story began on that cold February weekend. While America was locked in a chaotic world war, a young married couple found a brief refuge in each other's arms. By the time of my birth on October 12, 1945, a semblance of peace had returned to a war-weary world. I had been conceived in war and born in peace.

My father and three uncles each served their country with honor and valor in World War II. They seldom spoke of their war experiences, although all three uncles saw combat while serving in the navy and air force. They fueled my dreams with their patches and ribbons, which I kept as treasures in a cigar box. I fantasized about their service in faraway lands and on distant oceans, never understanding the underlying scars that war inflicted on each of them. They became real-life heroes in a childhood populated with television and movie heroes. Each week, I sat before a small black-and-white television and watched as Hoppy, Gene, Roy, and Superman assured us that Americans were the good guys who always fought for truth, justice, and the American way. I grew up desiring to serve the country like my heroes. I had caught the American dream and call to service. I was taught that it was a privilege to be a patriotic American and knew that I had the duty to carry the banner, and that banner was red, white, and blue. Early on, Trish and I would tromp through the house to stirring Sousa marches, and patriotism blossomed in my heart. Some years later, Sharon would tag along. I was proud to be an American kid, albeit one who was naively unaware of the forces moving rapidly against such a traditional worldview.

2

BALTIMORE

Today, the name connotes images far different from the city of my childhood. The Baltimore I knew, from 1945 until I departed for college in 1963, was a great place to grow up. It was a city of blue-collar families all trying to catch their part of the American dream. Baltimore was divided by ethnicity and color, yet it was a city of families and the conjoint values those families brought to society. Neighborhoods were proud of their distinctive values, traditions, and faiths, and they walked to neighborhood businesses, schools, and churches. Many neighborhoods were populated with endless blocks of two- and three-story brick row houses. Their white marble steps were a point of local pride, and families kept them scrubbed and gleaming. On humid summer nights, hoping for a freshening breeze, neighbors sat on their steps and passed on the experiences of the day, helping weave the fabric of friendship that held communities together. From age ten until college, I worked seasonal jobs, including cutting grass and shoveling snow, to supplement my twenty-five cents a week allowance. Throwing the evening paper paid two dollars a week in junior high, and graduating to the morning paper escalated my pay to seven dollars a week in high school. While attending The Citadel, I worked for two summers at a gritty steel mill doing maintenance on the rolling mills, and my third summer I drove an armored truck. I learned the lessons of getting dirty, sweating, and working hard, which many in America do for their entire lives.

Baltimore's rail yards, docks, and heavy industries cared little about color or accent. They were filled with the strong backs and muscular arms that made the city a leading port in postwar America. Yet it was a city caught in the shadows of Washington, DC, Philadelphia, and New York. Those shadows spawned an insecurity that manifested itself in a rabid support for its sports teams. The city loved the Baltimore Colts and the Baltimore Orioles. Both teams did battle against the storied franchises of greater cities, but they were our teams, win or lose, and their best players became local heroes. They were men who, along with their families, lived among us, sharing our values, community pride, and love for local beer and soft crabs.

Baltimore has its own distinctive accent. It is far softer than its northeastern neighbors yet certainly not a southern drawl. If you are a native, you are a "Balmorean." Yes, Baltimore becomes "Balmor," and everyone was addressed as "hon." A drink of water becomes a drink of "wooter," and if injured, you may call for an "am-bru-lance." Though many years removed, I still can identify a Baltimorean anywhere around the world simply by accent. It plays on my ears with the pleasing satisfaction of a familiar melody.

Our childhood home was on the northwest side of Baltimore. During the first half of the twentieth century, the community developed into a neighborhood of modest single-family houses on ample lots. There were abundant maples, oaks, and elms providing shade during the hot summer days and brilliant painted leaves that brightened crisp autumn days. They were arboreal playgrounds for the neighborhood kids, and many sported roughly built tree forts from scrap lumber.

Our two-story house had two bedrooms upstairs and a single bathroom and master bedroom downstairs, along with two living rooms, a dining room, and kitchen. The full basement beneath the house, with its rough-hewn granite walls, held particular mystery, which played upon my childhood insecurities. I was certain that creatures and danger dwelled down there. When Mom asked me to check on the laundry or some other chore, I learned to quickly ascend the creaking wooden steps four at a time, slamming the door behind me before unknown forces could pull me backwards into the darkness. I attended PS 218 from kindergarten through sixth grade. It was here we recited the Pledge of Allegiance every day before learning the "three Rs" ("reading, riting, and rithmatic"). With the Cold War blossoming, we naively practiced atomic bomb air raid drills by ducking and covering under our desks, waiting for the teacher's "all clear." With school only two short blocks from home, I was able to walk home for lunch. One winter day, with the temperature hanging just below freezing, the temptation to play overruled the urgency to return to school, so a friend and I decided to slide on a neighbor's frozen fishpond. After several minutes of fun, I fell through the ice into freezing water up to my waist. Scared of Mom's certain punishment, I returned to school with solidly frozen clothes and numb body parts. The horrified teacher immediately sent me to the office, where my mother was called. I should have gone straight home because her embarrassment upon arrival at school magnified my punishment. On the positive side, the paddling I received actually helped restore circulation below my waist later in the afternoon!

Baltimore is situated on an estuary of the Chesapeake Bay. Rivers and streams lace its corporate boundaries, providing natural shipping access to the bay. Surrounding the city were rolling, wooded hills interspaced with cultivated fields of corn, vegetables, and tobacco. Beautiful horse farms rivaled those found in Kentucky and Virginia and stabled such great champions as Man o' War and Native Dancer. Until I left for college, my life was bound on the north by Pennsylvania, to the south by Virginia, and to the west by West Virginia. Baltimore boys tended not to wander far afield. Rumors of cowboys, great mountain ranges, and canyons in the far west, beautiful beaches in California, and bayous in the Deep South were but dreams on the pages of *Life* magazine and *National Geographic*. I never expected to experience such magical places.

The mid-Atlantic area is a temperate zone with four distinct seasons where seasonal extremes were the exception rather than the norm. The one climatic trait that never seemed to vary was summer's heat and humidity. One could plan to sweat copiously from July to September. There was scant air-conditioning in the cars and buildings of my youth. At night, with windows open and fans blowing, you hoped for a thunderstorm or cooling breeze to allow you to sleep after an evening chasing and capturing hundreds of fireflies for research at Johns Hopkins University. Each season held the promise of adventure and excitement, but fall was my favorite. Multiple birthdays meant that Mom's baking

7

permeated the house with wonderful aromas. Flaming autumn leaves painted the city with brilliant red and gold hues when the temperature dipped to freezing. As leaves fell, they were raked into high piles along the curb lines. Local kids and their dogs always found time to romp in the piles to the chagrin of neighbors or parents forced to rake twice before burning them. As Baltimore's government became more aware of air quality issues, they banned open burning and sent large vacuum trucks along neighborhood streets to collect the leaves. When we heard the truck coming, we would bury an old basketball under the leaves and, from hiding, watch the vacuum truck suck it into the hose. A basketball was the perfect size to clog the hose and never failed to send the driver into a paroxysm of frustrated threats aimed at local kids when forced to stop and clear the hose. With the vacuum sounding like it would implode with an amazingly loud sucking noise, we would convulse until our sides ached while learning new words from the drivers best not used around our parents. Fall also brought the magical season of the Baltimore Colts. The team roster was filled with larger-than-life heroes like Unitas, Ameche, Berry, and Moore who carried the dreams and pride of our underachieving city on their backs toward greatness culminating in the "greatest game ever played," namely the 1958 championship game over the New York Giants. Fullback Alan Ameche and defensive end Gino Marchetti coached youth football a block from my house. Whenever they spoke to me, I felt eight feet tall. They were regular men with God-given physical talents who mentored a generation of Baltimore's kids. They became businessmen in retirement, opening several successful restaurants around the city. Colts fans never forgave the team owner for the surreptitious move to Indianapolis in 1984. Today, the NFL's Ravens rule in Baltimore.

Next to our birthdays, Halloween was my favorite fall celebration with its overindulgence in sweets and trickery. My best friend, Billy, and I would spend one night soliciting our favorite treats from neighbors and a second night tricking those we judged to be stingy or unfriendly. Typical pranks included soaping car windows and inserting toothpicks into doorbells to keep them ringing as we ran off laughing. For a few particularly special neighbors, we reserved paper bags of dog poop, which we placed before their front door. We then lit the bag, rang the bell, and, from the safety of darkness, watched as the resident would stomp out the fire. It never failed to please our juvenile minds. One Halloween, we graduated to placing stones in the hubcaps of parked cars. As we worked our way along a darkened street, I popped another hubcap free, and Billy put in a handful of stones. As I hammered the hubcap back onto the wheel, a gruff voice cried out from within, "Hey, what are you little jerks doing?"

Suddenly, the doors of an unmarked police car opened, and two of Baltimore's finest emerged very upset at being awakened from a nap. We ran into the darkness and easily outdistanced the two overweight officers, although their angry threats kept pace for a block or more. We both agreed it was another experience best not shared with our parents.

Winter would sneak in with shortened, gray days and the teasing of snow flurries. Throughout the city, the commingled prayers of kids rose to the heavens, beseeching God for more snow and cancelled school. When it actually happened, kids would fill their local streets and parks with sleds, and their excited cries could be heard throughout the city. Baltimore took on a beautiful white mantle that softened its often-dingy appearance, making everything appear clean and wonderful, at least for local kids. Dad never seemed to share my snow joy when he had to shovel out his car and put on chains to drive on slippery streets to the muddy rail yard where a cold wind blew off the harbor. Years later, when I stood in a cold, dark rail yard near the Los Angeles harbor, I began to appreciate the many years he worked in far harsher conditions to provide for our family.

One winter evening with daylight fading, I aimlessly prowled the neighborhood with a snowball in hand. I knew Mom would soon be cooking dinner, and hunger pangs turned my path toward home. With the headlights of an approaching car piercing the growing darkness, my teenage brain saw no reason to waste a well-made snowball, and I launched a pitch that would have made Nolan Ryan proud. Watching the frozen sphere arc toward the car, I belatedly noticed the driver's open window. Time and motion seemed to slow as I watched the explosion of icy snow on the driver's ear and cheek. Transfixed by my marksmanship, the screeching brakes and tires skidding to a stop on the icy road barely registered. Only the driver's screams of homicidal rage awakened me from my trance. The open door disgorged an extremely large man whose face, contorted by anger and dripping icy snow, stared directly at me. For a moment, my feet would not respond to the brain's urgent signal to run. As he approached with profane promises of great bodily harm, I began to run. The chase lasted well over a half mile. He couldn't catch me, but he wouldn't stop. His hate-filled screams bristled with a sincerity that kept me running. My throat and lungs burned from the winter air, and my tongue felt as if it would slap my knees, but I knew I couldn't stop. He had seemingly become a permanent fixture in my life. I prayed that God would save me from harm, and on I ran. Mercifully, the chase ended. Gasping to catch my breath, I had to return past the crime scene to reach the safe refuge of home. Under cover of darkness, I slipped tree to tree and down back alleys hoping to avoid his murderous ambush until I reached the safety and warmth of home. Mom's cooking filled the house with the promise of another delicious dinner as she hugged me and asked why I was sweaty on such a cold evening. I mentioned that I was starving, so I had jogged home, eager for her cooking. She smiled and tightened her hug until I slipped upstairs to wash and pray that the large, angry driver and I would never meet again. Thankfully, spring soon arrived to remove further snowball temptations from my mind.

Spring was heralded by a profusion of bright yellow forsythia blossoms, soft pink and white dogwood blooms decorating local yards, and the growth of new green leaves on the neighborhood trees ending the months of gray and cold. It was the season for baseball. The Orioles held court with the likes of Brooks Robinson, Gene Woodling, and Chuck Estrada among many lesser teammates long forgotten. It was the time to buy and trade baseball cards, and I had a shoebox full. Each spring I would buy nickel packs of cards wrapped with bubble gum, hoping for Oriole players that I could trade with my buddies on rainy afternoons. I couldn't wait for the season to begin so I could head over to Memorial Stadium on Thirty-Third Street, where two bucks got you into the splintered, wooden bleachers in left field. Glove in hand, I sat with friends, dreaming and hoping for a miracle home run catch. Dazzled by my glove work, the Orioles would sign me to a contract that would lead one day to the "Bigs." Such are the musings of young boys in springtime. My dreams of playing in the Bigs never quite made it past the Little League champion Howard Park Cubs in 1957. My zenith of baseball glory was documented by a team photo in the *Baltimore Sun*.

Another momentous event pertaining to baseball happened when I was about twelve. Several of us gathered with worn gloves, scuffed balls, and cracked bats to play a pickup game on a neighborhood lot. Tommy stole the spotlight with the brand-new thirty-four-ounce, two-tone blond Louisville Slugger he had received at Christmas. We all admired the unblemished bat, and each took a few swings with the hefty beauty while dreaming of launching prodigious home runs. After my swings, I handed the bat back to Tommy and turned to the serious business of choosing teams. A moment later, someone shouted, "Watch out!" As I turned, my head exploded into a profusion of bright stars and dancing lights that faded quickly to black. When I awoke, I looked up at Tommy and the rest of the boys through a haze of blood, blurred vision, and exploding pain. Crying profusely, Tommy apologized for having clocked me. His mother arrived and tended me until my mother came running. She, of course, screamed at the bloody visage of her precious son and quickly carted me off to our doctor, who diagnosed a concussion and sutured my left eyebrow back together. Later in the week, Tommy and his parents came over and handed me the bat as a get-well present. The bat's now long gone, but I believe that the best hit it ever made was the day it knocked me out. That same year, Tommy's family moved to Colorado. Several months later, I received a large box from them containing a beautiful gray felt cowboy hat. By then, my headaches, black eyes, and stitches had receded into memory, but the Stetson was worn proudly when the air force sent me to Denver for intelligence training in early 1968.

During early childhood, I had a season of mysterious spiritual dreams that left me exhilarated. They seemed to transport me into the depths of eternity where I felt the touch of God. Such dreams were too great for a boy from Baltimore, so I never shared them with parents or ministers. They were later replaced by a season of night terrors that filled me with dread and robbed the joy and exhilaration from my dreams of God. Unknowingly, the spiritual battle for my soul had begun. In my youth, I enjoyed serving the church as an acolyte and usher. During my early teen years, the minister encouraged me and offered financial support to attend a Christian college. I enjoyed the fellowship offered through my church until one seminal event about age fifteen. As Sunday services began, the head elder chained the church doors closed from the inside. Since I was ushering at the door, I asked what was happening. He replied that it was to keep some Negroes out who were rumored to attend. I was stunned that anyone would be excluded from a Christian church. Didn't Christ love and die for all? I was grieved and soon began to make excuses to avoid what I saw as the hypocrisy of church. It would have profound implications over the next two decades of my life. I bought into the foolishness that I was the master of my destiny and could control my life and that hypocrisy existed only in churches.

Following the examples of my heroes, I sought to serve America through a military career. With reasonably good grades in high school, I applied to West Point, but not being a gifted athlete and perhaps more significantly lacking political connections, I was not selected. The congressman suggested that I apply to VMI (Virginia Military Institute) or The Citadel to pursue my education. He said that if I did well as a freshman in either school, he would reconsider me for WestPoint. With Dad's encouragement in early 1963, I applied to and was accepted into the class of 1967 at The Citadel, The Military College of South Carolina, located in Charleston, SC.

3

THE WHOLE MAN

In early September 1963, the "Silver Meteor" pulled into North Charleston station. It had been far less than a meteoric train ride south from Baltimore, but it gave me time for the sad tears and fears of leaving home to subside and the wonderment of what awaited to flood my mind. Railroads of that era were bleeding red ink, and passenger service was an expensive afterthought. Arriving late, hungry, and tired, I stepped off the train into the late summer day and knew that my life was irretrievably changing. My first impressions of Charleston were less than favorable, and they changed little over the next four years. Charlestonians spoke with a rapid Lowcountry "gullah" dialect distinct from the softer drawl of most southerners. It required careful attention to discern their mumbled words. The city was segregated not only by color but also by class. "Old Charlestonians" cloistered in the area overlooking the Battery, where beautiful views of the harbor included Fort Sumter, an enduring reminder of southern failure. Though defeated in war, they never surrendered their carefully guarded traditions and lifestyle. Their beautiful antebellum homes often faced inward, guarding ancient gardens, only showing narrow silhouettes and locked gates to the less privileged passing by. The city had been spared Sherman's wrath in 1864, and the privileged clung to their legacy with a tenacity that excluded most others as unworthy, even Citadel cadets, who had once served to protect their privileged lifestyle from the "War of Northern Aggression."

Charleston's heat and humidity was Baltimore's on steroids. The damp heat sucked energy from my body as I searched through a pile of trunks and suitcases dumped on the station platform. It was weeks before I realized that it was not my sweaty body odor that provided the pungent smell peculiar to South Carolina's Lowcountry but a noxious mix of salt marsh and pulp paper from nearby tidal marshes, rivers, and mills giving rise to Charleston's economy. I stared at the city's quilt work of industrial and working-class neighborhoods flashing past from the well-worn backseat of a taxi. The driver's cigarette smoke and ashes showered onto me each time he flipped them out of his window. Approaching The Citadel's main gate, I was entranced by the dark, mysterious Spanish moss dripping from the ancient oaks in the surrounding park. It gave a sense of darkened foreboding to what lay just ahead, accentuated by a lion's roaring echoing through the park. I later discovered that the old lion's existence in the nearby Charleston Zoo was every bit as pitiful as a plebe's at The Citadel. Entering Lesesne Gate, I passed the somber stare of sharply starched, gray-uniformed cadet guards and caught my first glimpse of castellated white buildings ringing a broad green parade ground. On the four corners of the parade ground were weapons of war from each branch of military service, and two howitzers faced the length of the parade ground. Each passing building glowed resplendent in the bright Carolina sunlight. Several days later, a dark, brooding storm front passed over the campus with lightning flashing and thunder cracking much like Sherman's artillery on his infamous march to the sea. Chameleon-like, the sheets of rain changed shining "Camelot" into a dull gray world that would match my despair for much of the coming year.

In front of the main barracks with its soaring clock tower, sweating, gray-clad cadets greeted each arriving vehicle. Under their gaze, I felt a mix of fear and wonderment at what lay ahead. An intangible force had me in its grasp and was about to dominate my world for the next four years.

A shouted command rudely directed me to a line of sweat-stained strangers waiting to register. It was little comfort that the others seemed as nervous and unsure as I did. Parents and girlfriends fluttered about trying to say their last good-byes or to steal one last kiss. Surrounded by a cadre of intimidating upperclassmen, we were directed by shouted commands to points of uniform and equipment issue and finally, dragging multiple laundry bags, struggled to our assigned barracks. Before new roommates could introduce themselves, we were rushed to the parade ground where the rudiments of marching formations were introduced. The next destination was the barbershop where hair flew off like leaves in a hurricane. We reappeared hairless, nicked, and bleeding from the barber's thirty-second assault into the mutual humiliation of the plebe year. Our vocabulary was shortened to "Yes, sir. No, sir. No excuse, sir." We began recitations of "plebe knowledge" and learned the correct way to salute and a dozen more military fundamentals. There were somewhere around five hundred plebes in the class of 1967. I was one of approximately forty assigned to R Company. Following dinner on the first night, we were herded into an alcove room assigned to four upperclassmen who had not yet returned to campus. We sat cross-legged, crushed against surrounding boys, sharing stale breath and radiating body heat. Our mutual fear was palpable. Suddenly, the heavy oak door flew open, and two members of the cadre entered. We attempted to respond to the shout of "Attention!" but legs and arms entangled, causing many to fall clumsily into a pile. Neither cadre member thought it funny, and for the next several minutes, we were repeatedly drilled with "Seats! Attention! Seats! Attention!" until we gasped for breath, and our commingled sweat dripped freely onto the floor in the excruciatingly hot room. Only then did our company commander and first sergeant introduce themselves. I remember little more from that evening except the exhortation.

"Look to your right. Look to your left. Neither of them will be here by the end of this year!"

Frightened, I wondered if I was one who would fail. They also spoke of the special night yet to come when we would be officially introduced into The Citadel's plebe system. We had heard rumors of Plebe Night and wondered if this was the night they referenced. Could it be worse than what we had just experienced?

PLEBE NIGHT

The following night dispelled all doubt. After dinner, four companies of freshmen nervously assembled on the darkened quadrangle while upperclassmen stood quietly in the surrounding shadows. Over a loudspeaker, a harmonica played a melancholy version of "Home Sweet Home," followed by the stern announcement that the plebe system had officially begun for the class of 1967. The training cadre struck with cyclonic force. No plebe was prepared for the humiliation, physical challenges, and the painful emotional assault inflicted by the cadre during those dark hours. They attacked with the bloodlust of a wolf pack slaughtering an elk herd, until none were left standing. The barracks resonated with a cacophony of screams and shouts that befit an insane asylum. We fell under the onslaught until broken physically and emotionally. Filthy with the accumulated detritus of bodies pushed beyond their limits, we were ordered to double-time into the humiliation of a thirty-second mass shower, and then naked and still covered with soap, harassed back to our rooms. To a man, we crawled into bed broken in every aspect of that word. Several faceless cadets from R Company left school that night. Lest you believe I have exaggerated Plebe Night, let me assure you that it was far worse than described. Others would leave over the next three months until R Company was pared down to about twenty-five plebes by the end of the first semester.

Many of the training cadre spoke with deep southern drawls unfamiliar to a boy raised in Baltimore. It was soon apparent that accent and geographical identity were the dividing points of acceptance to those raised in the Deep South. Although Baltimore fell south of the Mason-Dixon Line, I wore the worst appellation one could be given at The Citadel. I was a "Yankee," placing me just below pond scum in the continuum of life. There was a distinct lack of southern charm offered to northern freshmen even though we improved the gene pool and our higher tuition helped keep the school in the black.

That year, I was often challenged by upperclassmen. "Hey, smackhead, what's a fool Yankee like you doing here ruining our fine southern school?"

"Sir, no excuse, sir," I said as my chin pressed my Adam's apple into my vocal chords in an exaggerated brace.

"Give me twenty-five, smackhead, and sing 'Dixie' as you pump them out."

"Sir, yes, sir."

"One, sir, two, sir, three, sir ... Oh, I wish I was in the land of cotton ... four, sir, five, sir ... old times there were not forgotten ... six, sir, seven, sir, eight, sir ... look away, look away, look away Dixie Land ..."

"That's terrible, idiot. You sing it like a Yankee?"

"Sir, no excuse, sir."

"Start over and sing it like you love Dixie!"

"Sir, yes, sir. One, sir, two, sir, three, sir ... Oh I wish I was in the land of cotton ..."

Though my voice and body continued, my mind wandered to another place and time far away from "the land of cotton." I was in survival mode and barely holding on.

The winepress of our freshman year caused focus on accents and geography to dim among plebes as we sought communal survival and mutual support. New friendships and even humor emerged from the mutual pain and suffering of the rigorous plebe system. One R Company friend was Pat Conroy, a leprechaun-like lad with an extraordinary ability to dribble a basketball and spin a tale. He was the first son of a legendary marine fighter pilot, call signed "The Great Santini," and wore the physical and emotional scars to prove it. The painful experiences from his childhood and The Citadel became the genesis of best-selling novels, including *The Boo, The Water Is Wide, The Great Santini, The Lords of Discipline*, and *My Losing Season*.

Pat documented how The Citadel of that era had the self-defeating tradition of trying to drive its freshmen athletes out of the school. Apparently being on a sport-training regimen in addition to military training and academics was not enough for some mean-spirited cadre. Pat, an outstanding basketball point guard, was singled out and almost driven from the school. Only the support of his classmates and the physical threats of a particularly large senior broke the will of Romeo's sophomores and juniors. His story and those of the plebes of R Company are chronicled in his book *My Losing Season*.

The Citadel remained segregated until my junior year. That exclusion often made sports teams mediocre at best and often the bottom dwellers of the storied Southern Conference. Blue chip athletes gave little consideration to the hardships of a military college in the Deep South.

Just under two thousand young men bunked between the confluence of the Ashley and Cooper Rivers. We dwelled in the maidenhair of swamplands called the Lowcountry, where we dreamed of forbidden pleasures while completely isolated from the fairer sex. It would be decades before the first woman would dare enter Lesesne Gate with the audacity to attempt matriculation. We were exhausted young men and often sat forlornly on weekends, working off demerits accumulated during the week. When we were able to escape to the streets of Charleston, young women would seldom stoop to the lowly cadet, especially one with a northern accent.

Some of my R Company classmates were jocks in high school. Their eighteen-year-old bodies were well muscled and hardened by recent seasons of hard practice and physical competition. I, however, cut a particularly imposing figure of male virility that demanded the respect of classmates and upperclassmen alike. Almost six four and 135 pounds, I was given the nickname "Stick." Being the tallest plebe in R Company meant hiding from trouble was difficult at best and a goal seldom realized no matter how hard I tried. Night after night following brutal sweat parties, I lay quietly sobbing in my jail-like bunk bed degraded in body and spirit. I desperately wanted to quit, but some force deep within kept me moving forward. I clung to one faint thread to home and family. Nightly, a train's mournful air horn echoed as it rolled across the Ashley River trestle on the track that bisected The Citadel campus. I knew that track led north to another southern town and connected to other tracks that traversed northward through several states and ultimately led to the rail yard in Baltimore, where my dad was working the night shift. It was an emotional connection to the love of family that sustained me through a year largely devoid of love. Love was not a commodity issued at The Citadel. It was deemed a weakness in the military system.

SIR, MR. TRASH CAN …

Life in the plebe system varied from the ridiculous to the harsh, at times with only subtle distinctions. There were certain areas in the barracks that were black holes for a knob. The stairwells, shower room, and the corner alcove rooms could be the scenes of painful discipline. I was well acquainted with the danger lurking in all three. One fine Charleston day following the usual lunch hall humiliation and starvation, I was double-timing upstairs to my room, dreaming of other times and places, when I accidentally bumped a large GI metal trashcan in the stairwell. The shrill screams of a nearby junior sergeant stopped me in my tracks, and I involuntarily braced. He punched my chest several times, knocking me roughly backwards into the stairwell shadows. His nose touched my cheek and ear as he vocalized my sin with breath that begged for mouthwash.

"Why did you soil that can by your filthy touch, smackhead?"

"Sir, no excuse, sir."

"Maggots belong inside the can, not outside, smackhead."

"Sir, yes, sir!"

To repent for my transgression, he demanded I apologize to the can and receive its permission to carry on. Uttering my first words, he rudely stopped me and ordered me to kneel and to shake its handle. After several minutes, my hope for even a brief rest before afternoon classes evaporated. A crowd of smirking upperclassmen materialized, apparently needing a new dose of plebe humiliation. I could see the innocent act of accidentally bumping a trashcan was rapidly deteriorating.

"Sir, Mr. Trashcan, sir, I am deeply sorry that I have soiled and offended you by my touch and humbly ask your forgiveness and for permission to carry on, sir."

As a dozen pleas for forgiveness went unanswered by the trashcan, I noticed the amusement of the crowd beginning to wane. After apologizing loudly one last time, I bolted for my room at double-time. My dash for freedom was cut short by outraged screams demanding to know who had released me. They pressed in for the kill, surrounding me as I braced for what I knew would follow.

"Sir, the can released me, sir. It accepted my apology and told me to continue to my room. You must not have heard while you were talking to your highly distinguished friends, sir." Mercifully, outrage turned into laughter, and after twenty-five push-ups, I hurried to the sanctuary of my room. As I reflected on the ordeal, I realized the can had a better personality than most of the upperclassmen I met that year!

Plebe survival necessitated remaining within the safety of the herd. If you stood out in any manner, you became a target for the cadre's discipline. Sadly, my freshman roommate was one who bore such unending attention with very little support from his classmates.

He persevered through the worst that the plebe system offered and then went on to serve his country with distinction, retiring as a decorated air force colonel. By the end of our freshman year, the plebes of R Company endured to become a band of brothers.

In our junior and senior years, we were promoted into leadership positions while learning principles that would be basic to military careers. We were inculcated with the warrior ethos of honor even as society at large was casting it off as an antiquated concept. One of my proudest achievements as a cadet was being selected by my R Company classmates to the Honor Committee for my senior year. We were tasked with enforcing the Honor Code, namely: "a cadet does not lie, cheat, steal, or fail to report an honor code violation." The simplicity of life under the Honor Code settled deeply within my soul. The last year flew past with rumors and stories of war in a distant land enticing our patriotic juices. The Citadel was turning us into its finished products, young warriors with honor.

During our junior year, the men of Romeo '67 received their class rings as we purposed to enter the "long gray line" of Citadel graduates who had preceded us since 1842. I was proud of the college, its traditions and its honor. I was proud to wear "The Ring."

ASHES

An unusual event happened my junior year. Shortly after General Mark Clark's retirement as president of The Citadel, his wife, Rennie, died. One Friday afternoon in 1966, we stood in corps formation on the parade ground while a small plane circled overhead. As cannons boomed, The Citadel formally honored Mrs. Clark's passing. While the band played, her ashes rained down from the plane, and startled gasps and laughter rose up from cadets until officers hushed the commotion. The event caused offense to some but amusement to most, and a normally solemn event was turned into months of sophomoric jokes. It's hard to imagine such an event taking place in today's society.

The first death of a friend also occurred in 1966, when Second Lt. Joe Missar, '65, USMC, was killed in Viet Nam. He had been an amazing athlete, scholar, and friend. He was the best that America and The Citadel had to offer. He died in combat shortly after arriving in Viet Nam. I wasn't sure how to process his death, so I filed my grief away and focused on my own growing aspirations.

THE BOO

Another individual deserves tribute from my Citadel years, namely Lt. Col. Nugent Courvoisie, USAR, assistant commandant of cadets for discipline (aka "The Boo"). He prowled the campus and barracks with the ferocity of a male lion guarding his pride. While his gaze could strike fear, his loud roar would paralyze an offending cadet in his tracks, from over a hundred yards. He was never found without a foul-smelling cigar clenched tightly in yellowed teeth. He delighted in nearly singeing a cadet's cheek with the cigar while he whispered with glee, "Boo! I caught you, bubba! You're mine!" as the cadet shook under the assault of fear and cigar-fouled breath. He was ferocious in his disciplinary role, but he was also a savior to many cadets troubled by life's vagaries. His wife received me graciously into their home one rainy night during my plebe year. I had been called from Baltimore with the news that my mother was hospitalized with a potentially serious brain condition. Through tears, I told them my story. As he signed my emergency leave, he asked if I had money for the train ticket home. The question was met with embarrassed silence. Without another word, he handed me enough cash to pay for my train ticket, taxi, and a meal. I'm glad to say that Mom pulled through, and I was able to repay him upon my return. He was a good man wrapped in a gruff, rough-cut exterior. He was the iron fist inside a velvet glove. He was a man of honor, and he wore The Ring.

HUBRIS

With our last finals behind us, we excitedly looked forward to commissioning and graduation. In early June 1967, we were honored by the Corp of Cadets' last parade and by the last strains of "Dixie" I would hear for many years. The Citadel seemed to have kept its promise to our parents: "Send us your son, and we will send you a whole man." We proudly saluted as the next generation of Citadel underclassmen marched in review. About 400 cadets from the class of 1967 grasped our diplomas and sailed our caps into the air. We were indeed the finished product of The Citadel, The Military College of South Carolina. Soon we were saying good-byes to family, friends, and staff, including The Boo. I saluted and shook his hand for the first time. He smiled and without dropping his ever-present cigar growled, "Congratulations, bubba. I should have run a bum like you off to Clemson. Come back and see me when you can. Be safe out there. It's a mean world."

"Sir, yes, sir."

Several of us newly commissioned second lieutenants spent the first days outside the walls relaxing at a nearby beach. We talked about life, liberty, and the pursuit of happiness while we smoked cigars, drank Southern Comfort, baked in the Carolina sunshine, and boasted of military exploits yet to come. We joked about taking out life insurance policies on each other while toasting long lives. I'll write about who drew the short straw in another chapter. I had become a physically fit young man far removed from the naïve, skinny boy who had entered four years before, but I was soon to discover that I was ill-prepared to face the harsh realities of politicians lying and friends dying for an ungrateful nation. This "whole man" would shrivel before harsher climes of life than the plebe system. It was a life kept at bay by the walls of The Citadel and the marshes of the Ashley River. Within those confines, an honor code held sway, and there was no dissent and little discussion of competing ideas. You were all in or you didn't wear The Ring. It had been a safe womb in the rapidly changing culture into which I graduated.

Diploma in hand, I thought I was ready to take on the world. All too soon, I would find that my hubris, like America's, would be crushed in the crucible of a strange and faraway corner of the world called Southeast Asia. As a young second lieutenant, I found myself adrift from faith and with a simplistic and unsustainable worldview to frame my new experiences. I soon found myself engulfed and overwhelmed by the chaotic and destructive force of war. It was a war that I later found lacked both strategic vision and a will to win by politicians and generals alike. It was a war never fought for victory, only for maintaining a status quo. As some of my friends and classmates died, I found myself enrobed in anger. For the next decade, it was to be my carapace, and it weighed heavily and filled me with dread.

4

It's Not Good to Wake the Sleeping Lion

The Citadel's walls and gates had enclosed an island of traditional values and behavior in a nation rapidly throwing off such mores. America, seemingly united under Presidents Eisenhower and Kennedy, unraveled under Presidents Johnson and Nixon. The national motto seemingly morphed from "E Pluribus Unum" into "sex, drugs, and rock and roll." Student radicals emboldened by a friendly press mounted a continuous barrage of antiwar and antigovernment protests, and I soon found myself in the deep waters of conflicting values. Following graduation, I received a student deferment to attend law school. When I entered the large lecture hall populated by hundreds of aspiring lawyers, I quickly realized that I had little in common and had chosen the wrong career path. Nothing during that first semester lit the fire in my belly. Law school was relentlessly boring, and I chafed under the tedium. In early 1968, I surrendered my deferment and advised the air force that I was available, expecting assignment to flight school.

The air force bureaucracy spit out an assignment to intelligence school at Lowry AFB in Denver, Colorado. The next eight months were filled with many good times and a bit of intel training often assimilated through bleary eyes and headaches earned the previous night. The Viet Nam War seemed far away from Denver, and the closest I got to the fighting was a dust-up with a senior officer for making a pass at my girlfriend in the Officers' Club. I explored the majestic Rocky Mountains while wearing the gray Stetson given me years before. I braved my first attempt at skiing and was seduced by the vistas and grandeur of the American West. Life in early 1968 was good for this Citadel grad while in a distant land a bloody battle raged at another Citadel in Hue, the ancient capital of South Viet Nam. The war had entered a new phase of lethality, and I was about to join as a newly minted intelligence officer.

In September, I received orders to the 355 Tactical Fighter Wing (TFW), Takhli AFB, Thailand. A few weeks of personal leave ended with tears and nervous good-byes to family and friends. As I left Baltimore, I wore a brave face but was unsure of what awaited.

At Travis AFB, California, I joined a long line of GIs boarding a passenger jet to the welcoming smiles and greetings from several pretty stewardesses. Going to war had progressed exponentially from the days of troop transports and long, dangerous journeys by ship. Onboard, it was unusually quiet with 175 GIs emitting more body odors than conversation. My fiancée had let me go that day with warm, sweet kisses and a promise to wait for me. My heart ached as never before, and tears threatened to unmask my false bravado.

The melancholy lyrics of "Leaving on a Jet Plane" danced through my mind:

"So kiss me and smile for me. Tell me that you'll wait for me. Hold me like you'll never let me go."

Holding her close, I joked that I would be fine and only had to worry about being hit by a bus in Thailand. I had no idea of the prophetic words I uttered. I was now being initiated into the brotherhood of the American soldier. In every war since the Revolution, soldiers have felt the emotional pain of leaving loved ones behind. I wondered if my fiancée would be waiting or, with melancholy turning to morbidity, if I would return. The lyrics left me with a deep sadness as the plane lurched skyward on its circuitous route to war.

It was unusually quiet. We were a group united in purpose and destination, yet each remained isolated within the thoughts, fears, and prayers of his own mind. We flew to Anchorage where our jungle fatigues offered little protection against the biting October wind and teasing snow flurries. Every civilian in the terminal wore flannel and wool caps, and apart from facial hair, it was difficult to discern between sexes. When it was time to re-board, we made the long walk back into a blowing snowstorm. Then it was on to Japan where a fuel truck spilled jet fuel under the plane. We sat tensely inside the plane surrounded by a ring of fire trucks. After an inordinately long time, we were cleared to depart. The lingering fuel smell in the aircraft cabin caused many to suffer nausea. Hours later, we flew into Tan Son Nhut AFB, Republic of South Viet Nam (SVN).

War remained distant and surreal until the hazy coastline of South Viet Nam appeared. The pilot ordered us to tighten our seat belts and hold on. We descended steeply in a military spiral approach, dropping thousands of feet onto the runway, followed by quickly taxiing to a remote location. Once stopped, our plane disgorged the newest American fodder into the killing machine of Viet Nam. Smoke arose in the distance where recent rocket attacks had hit. Helicopter gunships droned along the base perimeter, strafing the tree line for the unseen enemy. Nearby, there were people killing or being killed, and the war snapped into focus. The pilot's urgent voice directed those on board to remain seat belted for immediate departure. I tried desperately to remember the happiness of my months in Denver and the taste of her lips, but the memories shimmered just out of focus. A contingent of dirty GIs in jungle fatigues ran across the tarmac and boarded, bound for rest and relaxation (R&R) in Bangkok. They added new odors to the already hot, stale atmosphere pervading the plane. They did not speak to those of us already on board. Their eyes had a tired, distant look, and their presence made me uneasy. They seemed to know something that the rest of us were not yet privy to, and they were not inclined to share the secret with those not yet bloodied. As the door slammed, we taxied onto the active runway, and the thrust of four engines rapidly accelerated the plane skyward. We ascended sharply into the smoke and haze, leaving SVN locked in the chaotic struggle that was bleeding three nations of its young men.

The flight into Thailand was uneventful. Bangkok was a beautiful, bustling city that exuded a frenzied energy beyond that of most American cities. Only 465 miles from Saigon, it was awash with American military personnel, yet it was a city at peace. I was assigned temporary duty (TDY) status at a hotel downtown where officers were billeted and the food and services were top-notch. Two dollars bought a haircut, a beer, and a back massage. The city was both exotic and intimidating. Its people were friendly, and many of the women, striking. Bangkok hummed with life day and night and seemed to entice the visitor to partake of its many pleasures. Bangkok's only obvious shortcoming, by comparison to our Western system of order, was the utter chaos upon its streets. In fact, to venture there as either driver or pedestrian was to tempt an early death. I remain convinced that Thai taxi drivers were once poorly trained kamikaze pilots who had failed in their primary calling but were determined to succeed on the streets of Bangkok. I finished my first such taxi ride hiding on the rear floor, certain of imminent death. The war once again seemed surreal and distant as I sipped a Thai beer and watched the mayhem in the traffic circle beneath my hotel balcony.

A few days later, filled with nervous anticipation, I joined a group of officers and airmen crowding into an aging C-130 cargo plane bound to Takhli AFB. The morning was hot and the humidity already dreadful. It was Charleston on steroids. I sweated through my fatigues, as did every other man on the flight. We sat in webbed seats along the sides of the aircraft, facing inward, separated by pallets of supplies. I wondered what the men across the bay were thinking. It was a scene reminiscent of a poker game with everyone attempting to mask the reality of the hand they had just been dealt. Faces stared down as men studiously avoided eye contact or feigned sleep. No one spoke, but the aircraft's din made that a distant possibility anyway. The plane groaned and shuddered into the heavy air with its load of men and war supplies destined for bases throughout Thailand. Shortly after takeoff, the mingled smells of cargo and sweat were replaced by the sickening aroma of hydraulic fluid leaking from lines within the cargo bay. Smiling unconcernedly, the plane's loadmaster enjoyed the fresh air near the open bay doors. I tried to calm myself from impending waves of nausea by watching the tranquil countryside flash past just a few thousand feet below. Flooded rice fields glistened jewel-like in the sun while burnt sienna streams and rivers laced the land and flowed to the horizon. Soon we were on final approach into Takhli, a large American fighter base under Thai control. The Thai Air Force's aging F-86 Korean era fighters were parked neatly on one side of the base, and our wing of impressively large F-105 fighter-bombers, along with assorted support aircraft, parked opposite. As I deplaned near base operations, a flight of four camouflaged F-105s screamed overhead, banked sharply downwind, and flared onto final approach effecting a smooth landing. My heartbeat quickened as they darted past with drag chutes blossoming. I knew these pilots had just returned from the war raging in the sky over North Viet Nam. I wondered what awaited me as I hurried inside, seeking relief from the relentless heat.

I was assigned a private cubicle in a twelve-man air-conditioned, tin-roofed hootch. The latrines/showers were in another building about twenty yards away, necessitating late-night strolls to use the facilities. One night, half-asleep, I exited the hootch and immediately fell over someone on the steps. When we untangled, I was facing the business end of an M-16 held by a visibly scared Thai guard. He rattled off several sentences in Thai, and I replied in English. Thankfully he relented and walked away to find another place to continue his nap. Takhli was in west-central Thailand, closer to Burma (Mynamar) than Laos, and as base counter-insurgency officer (additional duty), I worked with the Air Police on contingency plans for base defense against communist guerrilla raids from Laos and Burma. During my year on base, there were numerous alerts but no actual attacks. During the wet season, monsoonal rains drummed on the tin roofs, making normal conversation difficult. During one downpour, my section chief asked if I thought the rain had stopped. Since I could barely hear his question over the drumming rain, I thought he was joking. Because intelligence shops are windowless, I suggested he open the door to check. He did and was immediately soaked from head to waist by the downpour running off the tin roof. I have never laughed harder at a superior officer than I did that day.

I learned quickly that second lieutenants were better seen than heard. My rank positioned me only slightly above a plebe at The Citadel in the minds of career airmen. Shifts were long and spent in a windowless building where intel weenies dwelled. There were charts, maps, photos, briefings, debriefings, and a constant flow of quickly outdated classified information to be digested and regurgitated to strike aircrews twice a day. Intelligence weenies were cut from a lighter cloth than the fighter pilots whom I briefed and debriefed. My exposure to the pilots was both exciting and exhausting. Bombing missions targeting the heavily defended industrial complex about Hanoi left them constantly tired, nervous, and hung over. Fear was their constant companion until the blessed day they recorded their one hundredth combat mission, which meant a ticket home. Pilots were best handled gently and were provided a shot of nerve-calming medicinal whiskey during post-mission debriefings. That calmed them until they could get to the club for serious drinking. Early in my tour, President Johnson halted the bombing of North Viet Nam (NVN), thus ending the "Rolling Thunder" air campaign. Our wing's bombing missions, however, continued to increase daily as the air war in Laos, "the secret war," escalated into full bloom. Perhaps a week after the bombing halt, my hootch boy asked in broken English, "Why are American planes still taking off with bombs and returning empty? Didn't your president stop the bombing?" Smiling, I mentioned ongoing training missions and, then deflecting conversation, asked that he not scrub my fatigues so diligently on the sidewalk. The deputy chief of intelligence (DCI) had already noticed several holes in my pants, and it was going to be a long year.

My parents and girlfriend also couldn't understand why I was not coming home. They, like most Americans, had never heard of Laos. The days settled into a monotonous routine that caused time to drag. We all had short-timer calendars divided into 365 parts. Each day, a small part of the picture brought you closer to going home. One day, I exited the shuttle bus with a throng of airmen heading for lunch. We crossed the main road in a marked crosswalk leading to the post office and base exchange. I assumed that the approaching Thai bus would yield, but screeching brakes and blaring air horn said otherwise. A dozen airmen and I dove for our lives as the bus screamed through the crosswalk, barely slowing. Thankfully no one was hit, but most were scraped and shaken. The driver was soon arrested attempting to flee through the front gate. The irony of the words to my fiancée reverberated: "Don't worry about me. I'll be fine unless I get hit by a bus." A few days later, the base commander circulated a memo to all American personnel of the need for pedestrian safety on base. My scraped arms and knees bore testimony to his memo.

The Wing's primary mission became the interdiction of the supply network in eastern Laos known as the "Ho Chi Minh Trail." It was an unpaved superhighway by jungle standards with an ever-increasing stream of men and material destined for SVN. Secondarily, we also provided close air support for General Vang Pao's Hmong guerrilla army fighting the NVN and communist Pathet Lao forces from mountain bases in northern Laos. Both areas of Laos became hotly contested as NVN air defenses were quickly ramped up as antiaircraft guns and SAM missiles moved into Laos, no longer needed to protect the ports in NVN. The ancient kingdom of peace became ravaged by violent struggle, and its almost unspeakable beauty was despoiled by our massive bombing campaign and NVN's open intrusion of men and military supplies engulfing the nation in violation of the Geneva Accords. Soon American pilots began to die in the jungles of Laos rather than NVN.

Days morphed into a routine of ten- to twelve-hour shifts with one day of rest. On a day off, several of my intel buddies and I took off by jitney and jet-powered canoe into north-central Thailand, exploring towns and hamlets far removed from the war's pervasive influence. Entering a rural hamlet, we were greeted excitedly by equal numbers of kids and monkeys. Neither group spoke English, yet both groups aggressively sought handouts from the *farongs* (foreigners). With children's screams and monkey chatter escalating, a nearby door opened, and a mature Caucasian man emerged, apparently annoyed by bedlam disturbing his normally peaceful day. I discovered that he was an American missionary living in the remote village. During conversation, he mentioned that he was from Baltimore and would soon be returning there on furlough. Further questioning led me to discover that he was going to attend a Forest Park High School class reunion and that he had graduated with and knew my mother and uncles. He assured me that he would share our jungle rendezvous with them at the reunion. Upon our late return to Takhli, we were greeted at the front gate with the news that we were regarded as possibly missing in action (MIA). We had neglected to advise anyone of our travel plans. We braced at attention during a royal chewing-out by one very unhappy DCI. Apparently intel weenies with top-secret clearances were not to venture into the boonies unless ordered to do so by those with far superior intelligence. I licked my wounds and smiled, picturing the surprise and delight that would light my mom's face at the high school reunion. It was indeed a small world!

The fall months in Thailand saw the weather transition from monsoonal rains to hot and dry. It was the season of the king cobra, and the base radio station gave a daily count of snakes killed or captured to encourage safety. The intense sun threatened to bake everything with its intense rays. One morning, walking to the intel shop, I happened upon a mummified lizard lying in the street. It had been crushed by a vehicle with its four legs splayed outward and rendered into the consistency and thickness of a well-baked gingerbread cookie perhaps ten inches long. Picking it up, I continued on my way to work. Refreshed by cool office air, I reasoned that it would be selfish not to share my unusual find with others—but whom? It would be wasted on my intel friends who were becoming used to my warped humor. We shared the building with the wing commanding officer (CO) and his staff, which meant that the only American woman on the base, apart from the nurses, sat just down the hall. She happened to be the CO's personal secretary, and her attractiveness had not been lost on this junior lieutenant, although it was well known that no one was authorized to touch. Suffering a lapse in judgment and hoping my treasured find would amuse her, I entered her office but found it empty. Only a tantalizingly sweet fragrance of her perfume danced on the cool air, cruelly teasing my libido. Disappointed and needing to get back to the duties of war, I placed the mummified lizard inside her desk drawer and went about my business.

Later that morning, I heard a woman's terrified screams echoing through the building, followed by the metallic crash of chairs overturning and the unmistakable sound of high heels rapidly echoing down the hall, racing her terrified screams through the front door. All hands ran into the hallway, and not to be singled out, I joined the throng. Almost immediately, the colonel emerged from his lair roaring profane threats of immediate and harsh retaliation along with court-martial to whoever had caused his secretary harm. He brandished the mummified lizard like a Mohican war club, leaving no doubt that he intended to taste someone's blood that day. He ordered all hands into the briefing room where we braced at attention while his raw tirade continued. He screamed that she was inordinately fearful of the many snakes and lizards commonly found on base and that she had previously threatened to leave her assignment because of them. I thanked God that I had not shown the lizard to anyone prior to this rapidly deteriorating prank. His gaze swept across the room until his stare settled hotly upon me. I kept my eyes straight forward, but he was not to be denied. He had the fine-honed wisdom of an aged fighter pilot. He had seen it all and done it all in three wars, and his tired, bloodshot eyes locked onto mine like a Shrike missile locked onto an enemy radar. He knew a smart-aleck lieutenant when he saw one. He also knew that none of his pilots would cross the well-defined boundary around his secretary. I sensed others in the room relax as his anger focused on me, the sacrificial animal separated from the herd. His exact words are lost to my memory, but they would still be classically profane in our modern world of relaxed morality. His hot breath, heavy with scotch and cigars, burned into my face. He was up-close and personal, and I almost reeled under the blistering attack. I flashed back to my days at The Citadel, when the piercing gaze and hot, cigar-fouled breath of Assistant Commandant of Cadets Lt. Colonel Nugent "The Boo" Courvoisie had often singled me out with the glee of a homicide detective finding his quarry. I had lived through four years of The Boo's hot scrutiny, and I resolved to make it through this episode. I silently cursed the lizard that had caused this entire episode by carelessly jaywalking on a base street. The colonel roared, but I stood firm. Because I wear The Ring, neither confession nor lies passed from my lips, only feigned surprise that the colonel could besmirch the reputation of such a loyal and devoted lieutenant posted far from friends and loved ones in wartime service to his beloved country. Intuitively, he knew he had cornered his quarry, but before he could strike the deathblow, the angelic sound of high heels again echoed from the hallway. She had returned, and with that knowledge, the colonel's wrath began to subside. Finally, he retreated, and with a few rear guard threats, he returned to his lair. I learned that day the wisdom of the African proverb "It is not good to wake the sleeping lion."

It wasn't until both he and his secretary rotated to new assignments a month or so later that I confirmed the suspicions of my friends. I gained credibility among both staff and pilots, and we toasted my newfound celebrity with beers and laughter while awaiting the arrival of our new wing commander, Colonel Heath "Bo" Bottomly.

My war was about to change once more. This time it would become personal.

5

I'm Dreaming of a White Christmas

Bing Crosby's classically melodic words echoed through the office as the base radio station contributed to my growing melancholy with the approach of Christmas, 1968. It was hard to concentrate on the war mission as homesick thoughts filled my mind. I missed my fiancée and longed for home. The wing had lost two fine pilots within two weeks. On December 8, First Lt. Bob Rex was shot down, and on December 21, Major Richard (Dick) Allee. Neither was recovered from the jungles of Laos until July 1996, when Bob's partial remains were returned to full military honors in the United States. Richard Allee's remains have never been recovered from the Laotian jungle. The mood at Takhli was somber as the holidays approached.

General consensus was that the wing would stand down on Christmas Eve and Christmas Day. Yet early on the morning of December 24, encrypted orders from Seventh Air Force in Saigon (MACV) indicated otherwise. General officers in the chain of command weren't about to trade sortie count for a holiday. A sortie was a combat mission flown by one plane. They knew that good rating reports and future promotions hung on sortie counts and resulting bomb damage assessment. Missions were flown in multiples of four planes or more to build the sortie rate. Wings and squadrons were rated on their sortie count, which was reported daily to the president, secretary of defense, and the joint chiefs of staff. If missions weren't flown, phones rang down the chain of command until someone was held accountable.

The morning missions were flown without event. Just after lunch, I stood at the podium while the four pilots of Panda flight and staff support personnel sat in the almost empty briefing room. All four pilots had volunteered so that others could have the day off. The weather officer attempted to lighten the mood with a forecast for "snow and reindeer" in the target area. He cautioned against confusing the sleigh with a MIG, eliciting a few polite chuckles. Flight lead was Major Dick Brownlee, a veteran combat pilot. Dick was a squadron executive officer, yet he found time to mentor and encourage younger officers like myself. During the months we had worked together, he was becoming a dangerous liability in wartime, a friend.

At the podium, I began the intelligence presentation: "Gentlemen, your targets today are enemy supply convoys and truck parks in the Route 911 complex west and south of Ban Karai Pass (Laos-NVN border). Air recon and ground sensors are reporting surges of motorized troops and supplies flowing through that complex. You will be working with a Nail FAC. You can expect small arms through 57 mm in the target area south to Ban Laboy Ford. No SAM (surface-to-air missile) activity was reported by morning flights, but AAA was moderate throughout Steel Tiger (southeastern Laos, along the NVN border). Apparently, the enemy isn't getting the holiday off either. F-4s from Udorn and Ubon will be working the passes to your east. Your TIC (troops in contact) call sign is Prairie Fire. No friendlies are reported in your target area, so if Nail marks it, kill it, unless authenticators are used! Check in with Cricket (airborne command/control) for continuing enemy SAM assessment and MIG activity."

Questions were asked and answered as updated AAA/SAM threat charts were examined and escape and evasion locations were suggested in event of an emergency. I finished my briefing with a smile, promising to personally call President Johnson if they shot Santa out of the sky. Smiling, Dick nodded and said, "I wouldn't miss it." The four pilots of Panda Flight left the briefing room for the short ride to the flight line where four heavily armed F-105s awaited. I wondered to myself if Dick had meant he wouldn't miss the sleigh or the call to President Johnson. There were quite a few men who would have lined up for the chance to give Johnson an earful about the snafu he called a war.

I busied myself with various additional duties while wondering what would be on the holiday dinner menu at the club. Holiday loneliness swept over me again like an incoming tide. I had suffered through a short-wave radio call the night before with my fiancée. How do you tell someone that you love them with the entire world eavesdropping? I expected to hear about my love life on the next "Hanoi Hannah" radio show from NVN. The call lasted three minutes with at least two minutes taken up by garbled echoing and static. "Hello ... hello ... hello ... I ... I ... I ... love ... love ... love ... you ... you ... you ..." So went the entire conversation with dueling echoes. The call added frustration to my loneliness. I purposed to overcome my melancholy by surrounding myself with friends and coworkers later.

The thunder from Panda's four afterburners shook the building as they departed on their bombing mission. I planned for their return in about four hours, knowing they would be hot, tired, and pumped with adrenaline. I unlocked the bottom desk drawer to ensure that adequate medicinal whiskey remained for their post mission debriefing, as authorized by the wing flight surgeon.

Perhaps an hour later, the loud garble of static and excited voices talking over one another emanated from the operations strike radio in a nearby office. Wandering over, I could hear several excited pilots, a Nail FAC (forward air controller), and Cricket (airborne command/control) all attempting to talk at the same time. Our cobbled communication network was almost as dangerous to American pilots as the enemies' air defenses and the challenging Southeast Asian weather. Too many people talking on too few frequencies was a constant hindrance to the safety of strike pilots. As I turned to leave, I heard words that froze me in place. "Panda two, Panda lead's down ... *static* ... I see a good chute ... *static* ... Beeper activated ... Coordinates are ... (garbled by other voices and beeper) ... bad guys in immediate area ... Start SAR (search and rescue)."

Within minutes, the room filled with pilots and staff personnel as the news spread through the building. We soon heard the welcome calls from the SAR team launched from NKP (Nakon Phanom AFB) en route to Dick Brownlee's location. The SAR team was comprised of two Sandy's (A-1E Skyraiders) providing close air support for two long-range Jolly Greens (HH-3 helicopters). Minutes seemed like hours, and the tension in Ops was electric. Panda flight's three remaining planes were ordered to leave the rescue area to refuel and then return to base. Simultaneously, we heard Sandy lead contact the Nail FAC as they entered the search area. Over the radio, I could hear the two aircraft systematically strafe and rocket the area, hoping to carve a safe corridor for the Jolly Greens to enter. The SAR team located Dick hanging in the thick jungle canopy snared by his chute, but they couldn't assess his condition. The surrounding area was reportedly teeming with enemy troops. The lead Jolly Green made several approaches attempting to reach him but was repeatedly repulsed by ground fire. Finally, damaged by enemy ground fire and with impending darkness, they were forced to abort the rescue mission. There was no doubt that I had just listened to a heroic action. I learned that day how helpless one feels when he is powerless to help another human in peril. Dick was left alone in the Laotian night. Dismayed and discouraged, I wanted to leave, but Panda flight was inbound to Takhli, and I would be the debriefing officer for three tired, frustrated pilots. To say the debriefing was difficult was the understatement of the war. The four of us made a valiant attempt to keep our emotions in check, but we had lost a good friend. It was made more difficult by the intrusion of Wing staff and other pilots desperate to hear details for themselves. Eventually, with frustration giving way to resignation, we adjourned to the club and the comfort of spirits other than the Christmas spirit.

The Wing's mood slipped into the grip of despair. I was one of many who considered Dick a friend. Late Christmas Eve, I left the club to the inebriated fighter pilots who had toasted Dick while trying to ease their grief and fear, as warriors often do when proven mortal. Alone in my hootch, I pondered the day's happenings. I thought about past Christmas Eves and the excitement they had brought in my youth. Yielding to loneliness and despair, I attempted to bargain with God, but my feeble prayers yielded no peace and seemed to bounce back from the ceiling. I promised to do something, anything, if God would grant my request for Dick's safe return. God remained silent. It seemed He wasn't in a bargaining mood that Christmas Eve, especially with a man who had walked away from Him in high school. Sleep danced just out of reach, and helplessness erupted into anger. I plunged into a depth of emotions never previously experienced. I wondered if Dick was having similar thoughts and fears while hanging in a tree in Laos that dark Christmas Eve. I wondered if he could see the Christmas star. I couldn't. The genesis of my unraveling began that night.

As Christmas dawned warm and clear, I sat alone with coffee and runny eggs at the club. The few officers present sat in solitude, seemingly lost in personal thought. There was no Christmas spirit evident that morning. I walked over to Ops and joined a subdued group of pilots and staff all sharing the joint hope that our friend would be rescued. I rechecked my threat assessment charts and wondered if I had missed the guns that downed Dick Brownlee or if it had simply been the proverbial "golden bb" (lucky shot). Guilt was gnawing at my conscience, and I wondered if others present were blaming me. The radio broke into the chatter of professionals ready to launch a new SAR mission hoping to rescue a pilot none of them knew personally. They were men who would fly into harm's way to rescue a brother airman. Looking around the room, I saw many more such men. I had taken their valor for granted until that morning. I remained at the edge of the group listening to the rescue. Dick's emergency beacon droned mournfully over the SAR channel, as it had the day before. Although he didn't respond to the radio calls directed to him, our hope was renewed when the FAC confirmed Dick's location in the jungle canopy for the SAR forces. He reported the area quiet and hoped to affect a quick rescue. We heard the heavy staccato of the A1E's 20 mm guns hoping to kill or intimidate any enemy hiding in the area, as their pilots reported their strafing runs by radio to the FAC. After several hot passes, there was still no enemy response. The lead Jolly Green hovered overhead, as para-rescueman Charles King attached Dick to the rescue cable. A wave of excitement surged through the room, and it appeared his rescue was imminent. Tragically, during the lift, the cable snagged on a tree limb and broke, sending both men falling through the canopy to the jungle floor. Though injured, A1C Charles King called for the helicopter to lower another cable and sling. There was no report on Dick's condition as King moved to retrieve the pilot. The Christmas still was suddenly shattered by a cacophony of gunfire that echoed over the radio. The trap had been sprung with deadly efficiency and threatened to destroy its target, the American helicopters. More American lives were on the line, and A1C King could barely be heard above the rising gunfire as he fired his M-16. The screams of enemy ground troops firing AKs could be heard closing in on his position. His last words shouted over the radio ordered his crew to leave the area to save their own lives—and then silence. The SAR effort was quickly called off by a general somewhere in a safe HQ compound. Beaten and battered, the brave men and their aircraft limped back to NKP, leaving one of their best to die on Christmas with one of our best. There was no Christmas miracle on December 25, 1968, as two Americans died in America's secret war. A1C Charles King was posthumously awarded the Air Force Cross for his heroic actions that Christmas Day. It is the nation's second highest award for valor after the Medal of Honor, and it would join the Silver Star he had been awarded the week before for a successful rescue also under enemy fire. Both men remain MIA in the jungle of Laos, the Kingdom of Peace.

I left the building empty, angry, and frustrated. I had a role in sending Dick Brownlee to his fate and had listened impotently to his failed rescue. I reasoned that the two lives lost were of far greater value than a few truckloads of supplies on the Ho Chi Minh Trail. I wanted to find and scream at the general who had ordered Panda flight's Christmas Eve mission. It had been a fool's errand but only one of many throughout the war. It was very apparent that Washington politics were hampering the American war effort and sacrificing America's young men. An inept military command, from the secretary of defense to the generals at MACV, added to the fruitless sacrifice of lives without clear strategic goals to win the war and without the honor to stand up to foolish politicians. My spirit was broken, and my patriotism was at a low ebb. Disillusioned, I began to openly criticize those in charge of the war, including President Lyndon Johnson, who I hold personally responsible for the war's tragic outcome and staggering loss of life. His direct political micromanaging of targets and tactics combined with foolish rules of engagement led to the needless loss of far too many American and South Vietnamese lives. It was a political war without honor for those risking and sacrificing their lives before a hostile American media and an increasingly hostile nation.

Tears glistened in the eyes of the men gathered on Christmas morning in the O-Club. Whiskey glasses were raised in honor of two warriors forever joined in death. I knew that this ritual was being repeated at NKP, where they also grieved that Christmas Day. As the whiskey burned its way into my stomach, my mind mixed portions of anger, guilt, and shame into a concoction of grief. It was a bitter gall that sickened me for the next decade. Death and war had become very personal, and there was no apparent answer for the pain I felt. From within my soul, the genesis of a deep rage scared me. My years at The Citadel seemed distant and innocent by comparison. My unraveling had begun, but sadly, it was far from complete. Christmas of 1968 easily remains the worst of my life.

THE SHORT STRAW

Good bosses know when one of their minions needs a break. In early February 1969, mine told me to get lost in Bangkok for a few days. He intuitively knew that I was wrestling with the Christmas tragedy. I spent the slow train ride south trying vainly to forget the worst Christmas of my life. Anger at the war's futility was unrelenting and seemed to follow me south. Another lieutenant from Takhli joined me on a predawn walk to the main post office where you could post mail and packages, make international calls, and exchange currency. By going early, we avoided the throngs usually clogging the services. I had called my parents and battled homesickness following our brief conversation. Dawn was breaking as we walked back toward our hotel in a light rain. We were the only ones on the street except for a traffic policeman dozing in a small street corner booth. The morning still was suddenly shattered by the screeching tires and blaring air horn of a speeding bus. Glancing back, I saw a large bus complete a 360-degree skid, jump the curb, and careen onto the sidewalk directly at the police booth and us. We dove into the street and rolled across the wet blacktop, joined quickly by the policeman. The bus smashed his booth and continued through a storefront almost disappearing into the building. A surreal silence startled me when the bus engine died, and I wondered for a moment if I was dreaming. The traffic officer dispelled that notion when he stood and excitedly tried to blow his whistle but only his escaping gasps of air sounded. His fear was accentuated by a large wet stain on the front of his khaki uniform pants.

Thankfully there were no passengers on the bus, and the driver was soon arrested, running from the scene. We continued to our hotel bar where a beer helped calm shattered nerves. Again I recalled my parting words to my fiancée, "Don't worry about me. I'll be fine unless I get hit by a bus." This was strike two. I wondered if there would be a third bus in my life

A day later, I sat alone in the dimly lit hotel bar nursing a drink, listening to a Thai band butchering The Beatles, when a familiar face walked in fresh off the plane from Saigon. In crisp jungle fatigues and green beret, he looked every bit the part of the American fighting soldier. Our greetings were warm and sincere. We had graduated together in 1967 and both wore The Ring. It was indeed a small world, and I looked forward to catching up on events since our graduation and commissioning. Over cold beers, we toasted friendships and compared stories until he said, "Bob, have you heard about Bruce?" I hesitated as a wave of uncertainty gripped my stomach. I didn't want him to continue, but he did. "I don't know the details, but Bruce was killed last week. His body has been sent home." Bill's words struck with the force of a bus—strike three! The impact of his death resonates in my heart today and will never stop until he greets me at my journey's end.

I flashed back to a carefree Charleston beach following graduation. We had toasted careers and boasted of future exploits, ready to take on the world. Surely, we were Uncle Sam's answer to the communist menace around the globe. His lips continued moving, but his voice became distant. I remember little else of our conversation that day, but the embers of my Christmas rage flared into full flame. The Viet Nam killing machine demanded to be fed, and my best friend had drawn the short straw. His pain ended in a jungle on January 26, 1969, but mine was just beginning. My anger was fed by the deadly impotence of our war effort and a growing desire for personal revenge. Disillusioned, I left Bangkok the next day and returned to Takhli. R&R had been a bust, but the prophetic words became very real.

THE THUD

Grieving, I lashed out angrily at those around me. Discipline and friendships were stretched to the breaking point. My boss tried to mentor me, but I kept him at a distance and dismissed his counsel. The intel shop was littered with the broken eggshells of my angry outbursts. I was disillusioned with the lack of honor among political and senior military leaders and the futility of our war effort and the continuing cost of lives. My briefings were tinged with sarcasm toward those in charge of the war. A few months later, frustrated with my role in mission briefings and the war in general, I had halfheartedly begun another strike briefing when Wing Commander, Colonel "Bo" Bottomly stood and glared at me.

Wilting under his glare, I stood at attention.

"Lieutenant, have you ever flown a combat mission?"

"Sir, no, sir."

"Do you know the threat envelopes for AAA and SAM missiles?"

"Sir, I can give you the threat envelopes from our intel books."

"So, you've never flown a mission or personally seen AAA, but you tell my pilots what to do over a target to evade their threat?"

"Sir, yes, sir."

"What about MIGs in our target areas? Have you ever seen a MIG attacking a Thud?"

"Sir, no, sir."

"Have you ever been shot at by a SAM missile or a gun that wasn't supposed to be in the target area according to you intelligence weenies?"

"Sir, no, sir."

"Ever have all of the above on the same mission until you're ducking into your cockpit resigned to your fate and wondering how you can possibly survive this war while trying to resist the urge to vomit?"

"Sir, no, sir."

"Lieutenant, I'm tired of your sarcasm and cavalier attitude toward our Wing's mission and my pilots. Do you think you're the only one who's lost friends over here? My brave men are flying and dying, and I don't want some smart-aleck intelligence weenie not giving them his best effort. Until you're ready to do that, get off my briefing stage. Do I make myself clear?"

"Sir, yes, sir."

Colonel Bottomly had made his point to all present. He expected 100 percent effort from everyone in the Wing. As I slunk from the room, pilots and Wing staff took a collective breath.

The rest of the day was spent in a fog of numbing humiliation and self-pity. Later that evening, I was sitting alone at the club bar nursing a warm beer and wondering what had happened to my career. No one sat within ten feet of my barstool. I was the proverbial leper who had just cried, "Unclean!" to avoid fouling those nearby. During my pity party, I sensed someone approach from behind. I ignored his presence until a well-muscled arm gripped my neck in a bear hug. The arm belonged to Colonel "Bo" Bottomly who quietly slid onto the next stool. He ordered two beers and gave me one. It seemed the coldest beer was always reserved for the CO. He smiled a toothy grin like a male lion testing the wind for an adversary daring to encroach on his pride's territory and said, "I was pretty rough today, eh?"

Unsure how to answer and wondering if round two was about to ensue, I simply nodded and took a pull on the beer.

"Want to fly with us?" he asked.

Now he had my full attention, and I quickly replied in the affirmative. "Sir, yes, sir."

Perhaps my anger and desire for revenge were about to be satisfied. The next day, the DCI authorized a request for my flight suit, search and rescue (SAR) pictures were taken, and basic flight equipment issued. I was about to go to war. It was my first chance to kill the enemy and avenge my friends. Most of my intelligence buddies thought I was insane to trade a safe desk for the dangerous skies over Laos. When I climbed into the cockpit a day later, I wondered the same.

The pilot's name and face from my first mission have faded with time. There were no written records of my exploits, since intelligence officers were restricted from direct combat flight over enemy territory. I do have a handful of fading slides taken on that first combat mission, along with my SAR photos and some quickly fading memories from that experience.

It was promising to be another hot August day as we met at the 354th Squadron headquarters in the early morning. Bison flight consisted of four pilots, with me as an "intelligence observer." We were assigned flight position four. Radio frequencies were assigned, tactics discussed, and ingress/egress routes plotted. Following coffee and a quick bite of runny eggs, we went to combat support for flight gear, including a survival radio and a .38 Special revolver in a shoulder holster. Next, it was on to Wing HQ for the intelligence, mechanical, and weather briefings. It was ironic sitting in the theater seats listening to the intel weenie instead of giving the briefing from the podium. The Wing's usual interdiction targets were to the east along the trail; however, that day we were targeted close to the northern border of Laos and China. Throughout the war in Laos, the CIA shop on base rarely shared intel with regular air force units unless it was to their benefit. Today it was.

A CIA special operations group (SOG) long-range patrol guided by Hmong guerrillas had confirmed U-2 film of a new road being rapidly graded out of China's "finger" jutting southward into northern Laos. They had already graded through the thirty-mile, no-bomb buffer zone along the Chinese border. This road was aimed directly into the back door of Long Tieng, the CIA's secret mountain headquarters in northern Laos. The road would enable the NVN to rapidly move men, armor, and air defenses into an area never before contested, endangering the war effort. General Vang Pao's army of illiterate tribal refugees were a people banished centuries before from both China and North Viet Nam. Their refuge became the high, remote mountains of northern Laos where other Lao ethnic groups shunned them as unworthy people. They were hardened by a life of deprivation and were used to fighting for daily survival. In the mountains of northern Laos, backed by CIA supplies and American airpower, their guerrilla tactics made them a worthy adversary to the NVN. The road, however, would be a game changer, enabling communist forces to trap them between superior ground forces in fixed battle. Our mission was to destroy the heavy machinery used in the construction project and to attack a reportedly battalion-sized force protecting the construction effort. The target was north of a small town called Louang Namtha, which today is a UN World Nature Site offering eco-tours to its exotic environs, which include rare birds, animals, pristine forests, beautiful waterfalls, and the bomb craters left by the "Yankee Air Pirates" of Bison flight. In reflection, I guess I can be proud that I left a mark in the world without destroying its beauty. Today, the finished road is the main paved highway in the area leading south from China into central Laos.

I climbed into the rear seat of the F-105-F (two-seat version) and, with the help of the crew chief, strapped myself into the cockpit. All business, the pilot gave a quick orientation of the cockpit with strong admonition to remain quiet and not touch anything except the ejection seat handles, if so ordered. He was clearly serious as he prepared for combat and not in the mood for small talk. I marveled that a plane so large could have such a cramped cockpit. I wondered if this day would be my short straw and whether I would be ridiculed if I climbed out. What had I agreed to? Perspiration flowed freely within my flight suit just from the exertion of climbing into the plane, and I began to itch in impossible-to-reach places. The engine started with the blast of a black powder cartridge, and choking black smoke enveloped the plane. Instrument and radio checks were completed, and taxi instructions received from the tower. With a salute from the crew chief, Bison-four joined the flight and taxied to the armament area, where munitions support men busied themselves checking bomb loads and removing fuse safety pins. We kept our hands raised in plain view away from arming switches until they finished their preflight duties. Once armed and ready, Bison-one and two taxied abreast onto the active runway. On flight lead's command, they ignited afterburners, and the two planes accelerated into the predawn sky. As they climbed, a bright blast of fire from each afterburner traced their path into the distance with the glint of daybreak to the east. Now Bison-three and four repeated the same procedure. As engine run-up was completed, the plane felt like it would literally fall apart from the thunderous vibrations of the engine. On command, brakes released, and the afterburner ignited. Thrust back into my seat by the engine's raw power, we accelerated down the runway and into the beautiful early morning sky.

Bison flight rendezvoused between cloud decks over central Thailand, and I watched a magical dawn break forth off our right wing. We were vectored to an aerial tanker where fuel was replenished. I was surprised at my sensory awareness in the cockpit. Flying at over four hundred knots, I had expected isolation from anything outside of the cockpit, but a quick splash of jet fuel washed over the canopy as we disengaged from the tanker's boom. The overpowering fuel smell necessitated use of oxygen to battle the resulting nausea. Crossing the muddy Mekong River, we entered "Indian Territory." We skirted the no-fly zone around Laos's capitol, Vientiane, where Laotian, American, Chinese, and Russian politicians pretended that Laos was still a kingdom of peace while joined in a dance of mutual destruction.

Our heavily loaded planes droned quickly north, occasionally bouncing on the thermals rising over the Laotian mountains, making formation flying a formidable task. I was amazed by the amount of air activity in the skies over Thailand and Laos. Tankers and command/control aircraft (ACC) flew in constant orbits of oversight. Flights of F-105s and F-4s flew from several Thai bases, attacking targets throughout Laos. Special Ops (SOG) groups flew covert missions from NKP and Ubon into Laos and beyond. Air America flew a wide variety of support aircraft from the CIA throughout Laos, transporting supplies and guerrilla troops into remote positions. Aging EB-66s out of Takhli flew electronic countermeasure orbits hoping to jam enemy radars tracking American planes. A myriad of other support aircraft flew supplies, personnel, and mail throughout the region. All were airborne and competing for radio time.

A flight of four F-4s from Udorn had joined us on tanker to provide MIG cap during our mission. Some friendly banter ensued between the Thuds and Phantom pilots until Bison lead commanded radio silence. Our flight leader believed there was a good possibility of MIG activity in the target area due to its proximity to China with its bases of refuge for NVN aircraft. Typically, MIGs would be vectored by Russian or Chinese radar to intercept the heavily loaded F-105s en route to their targets. Their deadly tactics often resulted in jettisoned bombs by the Thuds to enhance their maneuverability and survival against the MIGs. Thus, even if not shot down, the enemy won a tactical victory by denying bombs on target. Rumors abounded that some MIG aircraft were flown by Russian and Chinese pilots, so they would have combat experience again American pilots. The F-4s accompanying us that morning would hopefully keep the MIGs at bay. Our restrictive rules of engagement

(ROEs) made it easier for the enemy to attack by requiring each base to generally utilize the same routes, altitudes, times, and radio frequencies. I was now beginning to understand the high stress environment that our pilots faced daily, not only from the enemy but also our own micromanaging politicians.

The voice of the Raven FAC resonated with calm authority as he welcomed us to his "backyard." The Raven's lived at Lima Site 20A in Long Tieng, Laos, and were truly invested in the war effort. He clearly ran the show, and our pilots respected his expertise and bravery. Each Raven was a combat-tested air force officer now flying in Laos for the CIA. Flying multiple daily missions low and slow in an unmarked Cessna O-1 or T-28 over enemy territory was not for the faint of heart. In fact, Raven FACs suffered an almost 50 percent casualty rate during their shortened six-month tour with the CIA in northern Laos.

In the midst of a lush, green valley with Karst mountains rising sharply into the hazy morning light, a rudimentary track ran roughly south to north. It had been worn by the soles of many generations of traders and pack animals between Laos and China. From the north, we saw a freshly graded hard surface road emerging from the Chinese buffer zone. Billowing clouds to our southwest gave the promise of afternoon thunderstorms as Raven marked the target area with white phosphorous rockets. Following our flight lead, we rushed earthward one by one. The plane vibrated as it accelerated past five hundred knots, and my stomach struggled to keep pace. We pickled bombs and rushed back skyward under incredible g-forces, as the F-105's huge jet engine battled to overcome gravity. As we cycled over the target, I had to quickly rearrange body parts from the rude inflation of the g-suit following each bomb run. The g-suit was worn around the waist and thighs and was designed to prevent fighter pilots from blackout due to blood loss from the brain during high-g maneuvers. I was slightly nauseous but too excited to give in to the urge to vomit. As we circled back for the next target run, I saw what appeared to be white flashes along with streams of larger red tracers rising from the dark jungle trees near our target. Over the intercom, I asked the pilot what the white flashes were, and he calmly replied, "That's the small arms and automatic weapons fire that you weenies brief every day." I could sense his love. The multiple streams of lazy-looking red tracers arcing upward toward Bison flight and then falling away were Russia's deadly 23 mm and 37 mm that had brought down many American planes. Our bomb-release altitude was well within their kill zone. The war was now personal, and I knew that below, men were trying to kill us as fervently as we were trying to kill them. Our flight cycled several times over the target until all bombs were expended. Raven then asked us to strafe the jungle along the graded road where much of the AAA originated. In trail, we hurtled earthward, and each pilot cut loose with short bursts from the Thud's deadly 20 mm Gatling gun. Our plane shuddered and seemed to stutter as its gun ripped forth deadly explosive bullets into the jungle below, and cordite aroma filled the cockpit. I was thankful not to be on the receiving end of such lethal fury.

Mission completed, Bison flight reunited at altitude for a quick battle damage assessment before the trip home. The pilot of each plane closely inspected his wingman, and thankfully, no battle damage was observed that day.

Raven seemed pleased with our work. He reported several pieces of heavy machinery destroyed, the road cratered, and multiple secondary explosions in the area we strafed. We had probably ruined someone's day and given friendly forces at Long Tieng several weeks of grace. We bid the Phantom's farewell at the homebound tanker, thankful that there had been no MIG attack.

I was bone tired, sweat soaked, and numb from the waist down. As a result of g-forces, urine mingled with pooled sweat in my flight suit. My head ached from a pressure point caused by a poorly fitted helmet. I was exhausted, but I was also exhilarated from the combat mission.

Thunderheads, now bristling with the surety of afternoon violence, were carefully skirted. The radio chattered incessantly with other strike aircraft being vectored onto targets, tankers, and FACS. Airborne command/control aircraft tried vainly to orchestrate the entire effort, much as a conductor would attempt to bring harmony from his orchestra's many instruments. Safely back across the Mekong, Bison flight took the return opportunity to sharpen aerial skills as we hunted each other two by two. We chased among the clouds and then down to the deck, scattering water buffalo, until we finally neared Takhli. For a few quick minutes free from the stress of combat, the pilots simply enjoyed the freedom and joy of flight. Bison flight flew the approach with precision. As we flared onto final and touched down two by two with drag chutes deployed, just over four hours had passed. I recalled my arrival at Takhli ten months earlier, when I had witnessed a similar flight return from combat. We taxied through the midmorning heat to our assigned revetment, where a shirtless and well-tanned crew chief welcomed us home with a smiling salute and a thumbs-up. Four sweat-drenched, tired, adrenaline-fueled pilots had performed flawlessly from start-up to shutdown. They were truly "PACAF's Professionals," as their uniform patches proudly declared. My pilot quickly climbed out and walked around the plane, inspecting his bird with the crew chief. Exhausted, I sat in the rear cockpit barely able to move. Thankfully, the crew chief saw my plight and gave me a welcome hand down the ladder. Once on terra firma, feeling began to return to my shaky legs.

A newly arrived intel officer conducted the flight debriefing. The paper cup of whiskey brought my adrenaline and sense of excitement into check, but I needled him throughout the debriefing to the pilots' delight. Finally, it was home to strip off my disgusting flight suit and into a welcome shower. Dinner at the club was delicious, and the informal squadron party celebrating their newest "combat aircrew" went well into the night. Colonel Bottomly's smile seemed to light the room when he entered. Some bawdy fighter songs were sung, and several rounds of "dead bug" and "carrier landings" on the iced floor were enjoyed by all present. Boys will be boys.

A week or so later, I was inducted into the 354th Tactical Fighter Squadron and officially presented with the bright blue party suit worn by its combat aircrews.

In September, my budding combat aviation career came to a sudden halt when I was abruptly called into the DCI's office. Apparently, Seventh Air Force had discovered that an unauthorized intelligence officer had been flying combat missions. He told me that Colonel Bottomly had been raked over the coals by an extremely angry general. I meekly returned to my side of the podium, but my heart was now firmly aligned with the men who put their lives on the line every day, despite the meddling of politicians. Perhaps to allay my disappointment, the DCI told me to write up a citation for a Bronze Star. I thanked him but declined, saying many men had done far more without receiving one. I didn't want to cheapen an award for valor for those who had truly earned such recognition whether in flight or in ground combat. I remain in awe of America's valiant warriors.

Colonel Bottomly never again took issue with my briefings, and I will always appreciate the opportunity he gave me to experience war from a fighter pilot's perspective. I once again became a mild-mannered intel weenie, but I hoped that I would work for other men of his caliber during my career. He was a man of honor who led by example and was one of America's best warriors.

6

A Homecoming

The month following my last combat flight, I boarded a flight bound for home. I thought I was leaving the grief of war and its conflicting values behind as Bangkok receded into the haze. On board, the atmosphere was markedly different from the flight going to war one year before. Excited conversations and smiling faces abounded. The stewardesses seemed exceptionally lovely and attentive to our needs. One offered a friendly neck rub, and I almost melted from her touch. I can't describe my jubilation as the plane touched down at San Francisco International sometime around one in the morning. Bounding down the steps, I knelt and kissed the cold, damp tarmac covering American soil. Home at last! Hurrah!

Walking toward the lower-level entry into customs, I glanced at a crowd of perhaps twenty-five to thirty civilians gathered in the upper departure area. It was surprising that they would welcome us at such a late hour. Nearing the building, I read their protest signs maligning our character and service to America. No voices could be heard through the thick glass, but their angry faces and crude gestures left little doubt of their views on Viet Nam and those who served. I wondered at the level of hatred that motivated them to protest at such a late hour. Clearing customs, I had to run an angry gauntlet of Americans exercising their First Amendment rights, protected by the armed forces they so openly despised. Only my fiancée's embrace and warm lips kept me from a physical confrontation. It was my first experience with a nation that had changed dramatically in my absence. Family and friends were also uneasy with the war and the incessant protests taking place around the nation. There were few thank you's or even a simple "welcome home" to the men who had served. In the coming months, there were other confrontations off base that were unsettling and painful. The dream of following my father's and uncle's service to America was rapidly unraveling. I didn't comprehend the America to which I had returned, and I was deeply hurt at the senseless loss of so many for such an ungrateful nation. Strangely, I had become an alien in my own country, as my service was dishonored.

In late October 1969, I walked into a church for the first time in ten years. In my heart, I felt that I was being hypocritical by returning to a faith that I had spurned ten years before. After all, God apparently hadn't heard my prayers at The Citadel or during the year at war. I wondered, if God was loving, why had He let my friends die in a seemingly unending war? Why hadn't He intervened? When I asked prayerful questions, why hadn't He answered? Why didn't I get assigned to Europe? Why was He allowing me to be sent back to war a second time? Why didn't He care about my marriage and happiness?

Why?

At the altar, I took the hand of my fiancée, and we exchanged vows promising to "love and honor till death do us part," before a minister I had never met. It sounded simple enough, but at twenty-five, I would soon discover that I didn't know how to love a woman or to honor God. We made our first home together in Las Vegas after a honeymoon in Bermuda. The first few months were exciting and full of discovery for both of us. I discovered the magic softness and emotional complexity of my wife, and she discovered a damaged, angry, and insecure man. Even small events beyond my control would cause me to explode in fits of anger. Nightmares had become a regular part of my life, and I raged nightly in my sleep. She tried to comfort me, but I would not let her close. I was afraid of the man she would find and that she would stop loving me. I foolishly thought I would heal myself with time. Initially, the emotional wall I built was low, and for several years, we could still touch. As it grew, we eventually lost sight, and I selfishly surrendered my vows.

Air force policy promised assignment to one of my top three base choices following completion of a combat tour. I chose three bases in Europe, hoping for an exciting start to my imminent marriage. Surprisingly, I received an assignment to Nellis AFB in Las Vegas, Nevada. The last time I checked a map, Vegas was a bit west of Europe. I was assigned to a fighter-training wing as the wing intelligence officer. This wing was equipped with the new F-111s (fighter bombers) and, in another surprise, was due to rotate to Takhli, Thailand, by year's end. When I attempted to reason with those in the chain of command, I was dismissed with "Go back to Takhli, compete a second tour, and we promise you that we'll get you where you want to go after that." It left me with a decidedly bad taste in my mouth and disbelief of the veracity of those in the air force chain of command. It also put an immediate strain on my brand-new marriage. I responded with anger that permeated my marriage and career.

The F-111s, in a bit of karma, were grounded most of the time I served at Nellis AFB. Faulty engineering had resulted in control issues and wing cracks in this swing-wing, low-level fighter-bomber. While the grounding kept me stateside, it also resulted in a serious hit to morale throughout the wing. Everyone seemed to be on edge, and petty conflicts occurred on a daily basis, even as the war receded into the distance.

Living off base, I had no need to utilize the officers' club, which was the social center for officers on every air force base. It was apparent that Las Vegas had plenty of entertainment and restaurants to meet our social needs. My wife was now employed by a major Las Vegas hotel, and we were comped into almost any show we desired. Whenever I took my pretty wife to the club, there was a confrontation with a drunken pilot trying to hit on her. I no longer appreciated the rude and sophomoric behavior, which I had participated in at Takhli, so I resigned from the club. I was about to learn that logic and military life don't always coexist. The following day, I was being encouraged to rejoin by my wing's vice commander. He seemed reasonable and attentively listened to my explanation. When he handed me the form to rejoin the club, I politely demurred. One hour later, I stood at attention before the wing commander, a full colonel, and went through my explanation, naively hoping for his understanding. He dismissed my well-constructed logic and abruptly ordered me to rejoin the club.

Flustered, he shouted, "Why won't you just sign the membership paper?"

I refused with a classic, "Sir, no excuse, sir," and was unceremoniously dismissed by the now frustrated colonel. My officers' club membership had apparently replaced the F-111's mechanical problems as the top wing priority. Both of these men were career fighter pilots who apparently condoned boorish behavior by drunken pilots, even stateside.

The next morning, I was ordered to appear before the base commander. The general sat imperiously behind a large mahogany desk with walls covered by photographs tracing his long career as a fighter pilot. When I entered, he continued scanning reports while chewing the stub of a foul-smelling cigar. It was another déjà vu moment involving an angry man with a cigar. I stood rigidly at attention until I felt his eyes wash over me like a radar painting a bogey contact. He was direct in his approach to my sin. Shoving a paper across his desk, he gruffly ordered me to sign it, growling, "Every officer on my base belongs to the club! Why don't you?"

"Sir, no excuse, sir."

He growled a room-shaking, "Sign it, Captain!"

"Sir, no, sir. Sir, permission to explain. Sir, with all due respect, I cannot sign a contract or form I have not read."

He erupted from his chair with a roar and neck veins bulging. I noted that he was only a few inches taller standing than sitting. I took this as a bad omen, remembering the sour dispositions of many short upperclassmen at The Citadel who had once made life miserable for this tall plebe. They were mockingly called "ducklings," and we would be forced to quack at them, bringing their wrath upon us to the delight of our taller cadre. An older duckling was now on the attack, and I thought momentarily of answering him with a "quack." I also recalled the colonel at Takhli who thought he had lost his secretary to a mummified lizard and had angrily targeted my cheek with his cigar. My mind enjoyed the humor for a brief millisecond, before I was roughly jolted back to the present. His fists were white-knuckled as he banged on the mahogany desk, and raising the ante, he screamed, "Don't you want to be an air force officer?"

The cigar glowed brightly from the rush of air carrying his scream. I thought of The Citadel and how Assistant Commandant, Lt. Colonel Nugent "The Boo" Courvoise's roaring voice and foul cigar had prepared me for a moment such as this. I withstood the blast and replied, "Sir, yes, sir. Sir, permission to explain, sir."

His response emanated from somewhere deep within and nearly caused his cigar to spontaneously burst into flame with a color matching his bright red complexion. Cursing me with a roar that shook the pictures on his office walls, he again screamed, "Don't you want to be an air force officer?"

Somewhere in the deep recesses of my mind, I understood that I had passed a point of no return. There would be no confession or absolution before this man. I knew that my calling to serve America that I had excitedly begun two years before was disintegrating before my eyes. Looking directly into his eyes, I calmly replied, "Sir, if that means I have to emulate you, then no, sir, I guess I don't want to be an air force officer."

There may have been a small thermonuclear explosion somewhere in his bowels. His outraged obscenities brought his aide running, and I was unceremoniously ushered onto the front street, shaken by the day's events.

News of my insubordination beat me back to the wing office, where a troubled colonel called me in and vainly sought to counsel me against my decision. Tired of trying to reason with unreasonable people, I decided that if the air force wanted to shoot me down, I wouldn't go without a fight. I told the CO that I was right to protect my wife and would not rejoin now if they named the club after me. I thought the mismanaged war had been left far behind, but in the coming months, I would see more combat than I had in Laos. The sad truth of this war was it would all be "friendly fire," and it was directed at me. Even one of the colonel's wives got in on the fun. My wife asked me to pick up a half gallon of milk on the way home, so I ran by the commissary. It was a blazingly hot afternoon, and every parking spot was taken except for a half dozen reserved for colonels and generals immediately in front of the entrance. I circled the lot several times before I gave in to temptation and parked in one of the colonel's spots. I was in the store less than five minutes. Upon exiting, a large Chrysler with tinted windows was parked blocking my egress. As I approached, the driver's window lowered, and a stern-faced mature woman asked coldly, "Captain, are you a colonel?" I replied with the obvious, "No, ma'am, I'm a captain," while carefully covering my name tag with the milk carton.

"Then, Captain, why are you parked in my reserved space?"

"Excuse me, ma'am, but are you a colonel?"

"How dare you speak to me that way? My husband's a colonel, and he's going to hear about this!"

"Yes, ma'am, I'm sure he will. But since this is an air force base, and I'm a captain and you're a civilian dependent, I outrank you, so please move your car, and I'll be out of your way."

She moved, and I hastily left the base before an angry colonel could call the air police at the back gate. My wife and I traded cars for the next month, and I made sure not to shop at the commissary for a long time.

Going to the base every day became drudgery. I was given many additional duties and found the stateside military more petty than the air force at war. Other wing officers had been ordered to avoid me under threat of damaging their own careers. Only the enlisted men at my intelligence shop supported me. I won't bore you with the minutia of an angry bureaucracy attempting to destroy one of its own; however, there was one classic attempt to set me up that I will relate.

During my last six months in service, I was unexpectedly assigned as Nellis AFB's top secret control officer. This position was normally held by someone above my junior captain rank. As I dug into the manuals delineating the duties of the position, I learned from a friend that an inspector general's (IG) visit was only days away. I quickly discovered that the position had been mishandled by my predecessors and that several top-secret documents were missing or misplaced, along with many irregularities in the handling of the wing's classified documents. I typed a report of my findings and requested a full inquiry by wing staff and the IG into the deficient handling of those previously tasked with classified control and the command staff responsible for their oversight. Members of the wing staff were copied along with the base commanding general. I hand-carried the original report to the IG team that arrived on base a day or so later, despite having been ordered to avoid them. Mysteriously, the reports I sent through the chain of command vanished, but the copy I personally handed to the IG team leader, thankfully, did not. It saved my bacon from an obvious attempt to set me up for a court-martial. The IG team leader and the wing CO went nose to nose in his office. As Desi once famously said, "Loosey, you got some 'splaning to do!"

The target was taken off my back at that time, but it was clearly time to leave the air force. Daily frustrations at the base bled over into my home life, robbing us of marital peace and harmony. I suggested we relocate to Denver where we had met, courted, and enjoyed many happy times just a few short years before. I reasoned that it would be our chance for a fresh start, and perhaps we could find the elusive happiness that always seemed just out of my reach. My wife desired to return to the Los Angeles area, where family and friends offered support. She contemplated a return to flying as a stewardess and thought she could hold a position in LA. I relented and randomly began seeking employment in Southern California. My understanding of the American dream was morphing into something beyond my control, and I was being swept along by events. My military career had failed miserably, and I wondered what lay ahead.

I guess it's true, "What happens in Vegas stays in Vegas." Almost everything, that is, except for my anger.

As we drove west from Las Vegas in January 1972, I thought I heard a general faintly screaming "good riddance" in the distance, but it could have just been the cold desert wind blowing at my back.

I smiled and uttered, "Sir, no excuse, sir."

7

To Protect and to Serve

We drove through the beautifully rugged desert between Las Vegas and Los Angeles, chasing the sun westward to the Pacific Ocean. My wife had agreed to live near the beach to entice me to Los Angeles. We settled into a small condo two blocks from the sand in Playa Del Rey between the Los Angeles Airport and Venice Beach. When the evening rush quieted, the breaking waves sounded as if they might flood our condo. During the daytime, the cacophony of several million urban souls moving about trumped the beach music. I soon became part of that chaotic noise. Los Angeles was a sprawl of smaller cities and neighborhoods that had grown together. While most East Coast cities grew upward, Los Angeles grew outward. I had difficultly getting my directional bearings. One could drive in three directions to hit the Pacific Ocean. Streets and towns had strange-sounding and, to me, unpronounceable names, such as La Cienega, Sepulveda, La Tijera, La Canada, Tujunga, and many more rooted in its Mexican culture. Most East Coast cities had a decided blue-collar rough edge to them, but Los Angeles was glitz and glamour where money talked and status ruled from gated West Side communities while pretending the barrios of East Los Angeles and South Central didn't exist. The metropolitan area was also choked with traffic and smog, as the pollution hung in the ring of surrounding mountains. On a clear winter day following a storm, the view of palm trees and green hills framed by snowcapped mountains was without equal in America. Unfortunately, the storms were few, and unhealthful yellow air often smothered Southern California's natural beauty.

I was accepted into the LAPD academy class of March 1972. The hiring process had been quick and easy given my service credentials and degree. Flattered by the LAPD's national renown and its solicitous attention, I soon found that I had naively traded one traditional-values-based organization for another. Without the innate calling needed to make a successful career as a cop, I careened along the path of least resistance. The academy was nestled in a narrow ravine opposite Dodger Stadium, surrounded by the steep hills of Elysian Park. Its gymnasium was an ancient, hot structure constructed for boxing in the 1932 Olympics. On the first day, I stood at attention among several ranks of business-suited recruits numbering approximately 110 men. The LAPD academy instructors prowling about were menacingly fit and not to be taken lightly.

The cadre member berated a nearby recruit's haircut, who responded with a curse, followed by, "I'm not cutting my hair for you!" and he stomped out of our briefly commingled lives. His retreating footsteps echoed loudly on the wooden floor, and for a moment, I wondered if I should follow. Several instructors did, I'm sure to assist him off campus.

The next five months were an immense physical challenge. Through grueling physical training and daily runs in the surrounding hills, we were pushed to exhaustion and then forced to give more. I quickly dropped in weight from 220 to 185 pounds. At age twenty-seven, I was hit with the moniker "Grandpa" by some of the younger recruits. The five months flashed past as I acquired the skills and techniques designed to save a cop's life on the mean streets of Los Angeles. We practiced marksmanship daily with a .38 revolver and 12-gauge shotgun. I learned baton techniques and combat wrestling along with pain compliance and chokeholds. One classmate fell asleep during a short film in an officer survival class. The instructor choked him unconscious in front of the class and dragged him outside to recover. His point made, officer survival was never taken lightly by those remaining. The humiliated recruit involuntarily left the academy that day. As the months passed, I perceived my wife becoming more uneasy about my career choice. Even as I learned to assertively deal with criminals, I became more defensive and uncertain about our marriage. I was learning street jargon to speak to hoodlums but was unable to speak from my heart to my wife. The LAPD was not into marriage counseling.

Once passive and nonconfrontational, I began to walk with the swagger of self-assurance that marked the "old school" LAPD. There were fewer than 6,800 sworn police officers to police a city of 470 square miles in size. On any given night shift, there were seldom more than 350 officers on the streets. Los Angeles's incredible diversity made police work a challenge, as the demographics began to rapidly shift both ethnically and politically. My academy class was one of the last to receive the rank and badge of "policeman" from then deputy chief Daryl Gates. In 1973, the badge changed to "police officer," and women began entering the ranks on equal footing with their male counterparts. The LAPD continued to slowly evolve, trying to keep the peace in a rapidly changing society.

VENICE

My first patrol assignment was in Venice Division, close to home, but a world away in the demographics of counterculture. Groups protesting everything traditional in American culture could be found in this eclectic beach town, where many of society's traditional values were cast aside as archaic. Residents included the extremely wealthy and extreme groups that hated the wealthy. Among these groups were the Black Panthers, Students for a Democratic Society (SDS), Symbionese Liberation Army (SLA), black and Hispanic gangs, and a 1 percent outlaw motorcycle gang. Venice also had black and Hispanic ghettos, a Russian Jewish ghetto, Muscle Beach, street entertainers, conmen, a hippy drug culture, and tourists all mingling day and night. It was a great place to be a cop, and I was never bored a single day. I received a rich street education to supplement the academy instruction.

A homicide call came during my first week of patrol duty. Working a two-man car, we received a code three call: "Fourteen Adam Six, shots fired, man down, possible suspect at scene. Fourteen Adam Six, handle code three. Unit to back identify." Parking several buildings away and with guns drawn, we cautiously ascended the stairs to the second-story apartment, hoping backup would soon arrive. Classroom scenarios raced through my mind, and I hoped that I wouldn't react foolishly in front of my training officer. Through an open door, women's voices wailed hysterically, crying out to God in grief-filled prayer. We carefully opened the screen door and saw a shirtless, African American man lying on his back on the living room floor. I noticed four or five small bullet holes scattered about the victim's abdomen and chest but little blood. He looked asleep, and I almost expected him to awaken and sit up. The women continued to wail, ignoring us until my partner interrupted the chorus long enough to learn that there was no outstanding murder suspect. Indeed, she sat front and center on the sofa with her sisters on either side. Through copious tears, she confessed that she had shot her husband after she caught him with another woman. She confessed with simple eloquence, "I told him that I'd shoot him if he cheated on me, and I done shot him. O Lordy, please forgive me. I love him, but I done killed him."

My salty training officer quietly whispered a comment about her poor shot pattern. It was my introduction to a police coping mechanism, namely a jaded sense of humor when confronting the vagaries of life and death. A .22-caliber rifle leaned in the corner, its barrel still warm from having been recently fired. We notified division homicide, and they gladly handled the open-shut case. As we transported the wife to jail, I naively wondered if all murders would be this easy to handle. Maybe Dragnet and Adam-12 were true after all.

A few days later, we received a "fight call" at Muscle Beach. Upon arrival, I observed a crowd gathered around the workout area, laughing at an individual nursing a bloody nose. He was apparently the loser in a one-sided fight over use of exercise equipment. The massive suspect stood nearby, defiantly awaiting our arrival, with tautly oiled muscles glistening in the sunlight. My astute training officer ordered me to cuff him while he checked on the injured party. The crowd was anxiously awaiting round two, where they anticipated a police officer being screwed face-first into the nearby sand. I quietly approached the suspect, tossed him my cuffs, and with a calm voice asked that he put them on. He refused and, with muscles flexing in anticipation, seemed anxious to commence another beating. I unsnapped my holster and placed my hand on my .38 saying, "We're not going to fight. You can either comply, or I'll shoot before you can reach me."

He stood before me as a bull before a matador. He finally relented and, much to my relief, put on the cuffs and walked quietly to our black and white. Judging from the comments flying from the cowards in the crowd, there was a general disappointment that peace had returned without further bloodshed. They soon dispersed, drifting along Ocean Front Walk in search of more free entertainment at others' expense. From that arrest, I learned that a good bluff helps make an effective policeman. I would also soon learn that some on the street will call that bluff, and a cop had better be ready.

A BEACH PARTY

July Fourth bought teeming crowds from the inner city for a frolicking day at Dockweiler Beach. It wasn't long before fights broke out, and several bike riders were assaulted and robbed. Shortly after those incidents, a vicious gang rape occurred on the beach, and all of Venice Division responded to multiple assistance calls from overwhelmed units. A tactical alert was called in West Bureau, where urban chaos had interrupted the typically mellow California beach scene.

My wife and family were barbecuing as we sped through Playa Del Rey with sirens screaming. I yearned to be with them enjoying the holiday like normal folks. The coming hours would reinforce that yearning in spades.

I joined approximately twenty-five or thirty uniformed personnel formed in a tight defensive circle on the beach. We stood shoulder to shoulder with batons at ready facing the encircling crowd of hundreds. Curses, bottles, firecrackers, and beer cans rained down, and several agitators in the crowd, smelling blood, urged a full assault on our small group of "pigs." Fear sought to overwhelm my training, and I reflected on my relatively short life now flashing before my eyes. Had I survived a year at war only to be killed at the beach on the most American of holidays? I had seen this situation in a dozen cowboy movies, and it seldom ended well for the small circle of defenders. One city lifeguard foolishly attempted to drive through the crowd to reach our position, but his truck was quickly overturned. He was beaten and forced to run for his life. I pondered my sanity for having sworn to "protect and serve" the people of Los Angeles. Nothing in the academy had prepared me for this riotous moment, and I doubted that I would survive the day.

Before I could totally surrender to my fear, I witnessed how a few brave, well-trained men could control a mob. The sergeant standing in our midst had identified the most vocal instigators in the mob. He formed a flying wedge with six officers who surged into the crowd, grabbing the three agitators. Just as quickly, they were back inside our defensive circle with the suspects cuffed facedown in the sand. Within minutes, the mob, having lost its most bellicose leaders and collective nerve, began to back down. The sergeant had also radioed for traffic personnel to write violations on the hundreds of vehicles illegally parked along the beachfront road. The crowd quickly dispersed as most ran to their cars hoping to avoid tickets, vehicle impounds, and a long walk home. Training and tactics had trumped mob mentality. I was duly impressed, yet I yearned to be at the family's barbecue enjoying a cold beer and a good burger. I also hoped this wasn't a yearly Los Angeles holiday tradition.

THE WEST SIDE

My next assignment was West Los Angeles Division, where extreme wealth wreaked havoc with human values, and entitlement based on that wealth was an assumed right. I rubbed shoulders with stars of TV and movies and found some, like Charleston Heston, Jack Webb, and Sammy Davis Jr., supportive of law enforcement. Sadly, the same could not be said for many others. As a new policeman, I began to perceive that many people did not care for the LAPD's core values of "protection and service." In fact, most wanted to be left alone in their pursuit of happiness, greed, addictions, and predation. I began to view human society from a new perspective, and it opened my eyes to reality. I had naively assumed that most people lived and shared my values. While some did, many did not, and it bred trouble with a capital T on the streets of Los Angeles.

Among many calls handled, a few stand out. One night working patrol, we received a "bomb threat and possible suspect on scene" at a local synagogue following midweek services. Radical groups were raising the bar with terror threats in Los Angeles, and we knew this was potentially serious. As two officers combed the darkened sanctuary on the first floor, my partner and I descended darkened stairs to the basement classrooms. We each searched in different directions off the central hallway, losing sight of one another in the darkness. Clearing several rooms with flashlight and gun at the ready, I opened yet another door into a small room. I saw a man with a flashlight holding a gun. Startled, I jumped aside and almost fired, until I realized that I was looking into a full-length dressing mirror. The man with the flashlight and gun was me! I laughed quietly to myself while catching my breath. Minutes later, my partner approached and asked what was left to search. I motioned toward the door and told him I had his back. He opened the door, hit the room with his light, and gasping, fell back into the hallway. I laughed so hard that he threatened to shoot me. But it got even better when a sergeant arrived to supervise our search efforts. We heard him coming down the steps and quickly closed the door. After a quick update, we asked him to check that room while we cleared another one down the hall. With flashlight and gun in hand, he opened the door. For the third time in minutes, a loud gasp of fright followed by laughter rang out as another cop almost shot his own reflection. The red-faced sergeant left us alone the rest of the shift.

On a quiet Sunday morning, we cruised the tony neighborhoods north of Wilshire Boulevard surrounded by great homes built to display the wealth and power of their owners. We were flagged to the curb by a male nurse in white scrubs. He asked that we search the large, single-story house before us for the elderly home owner. He had been unable to reach her for days, and she wouldn't answer phone calls or the doorbell. We were a bit irritated at being interrupted in our lazy morning but agreed to search. There was no response to our knocks front or rear and no sign of life through the windows. We were able to easily jimmy the rear screen door latch and entered the kitchen. Uneaten food lay covered by green mold in a skillet on the stove. Filthy plates and cooking utensils covered every inch of counter space, and roaches scurried at our approach. There was no answer to our shouts, "Police! LAPD! Is anyone here?" Entering the large living room, we found it choked floor to ceiling with piled furniture. The nurse mentioned that the couple had been auctioneers and hoarded great amounts of home furnishings before her husband's death. There was scarcely room to move throughout the house, which appeared more a warehouse than a residence. We carefully searched each room until only the bedrooms remained. My partner ordered me to search the master bedroom while he checked down the hall. We both knew that if she was in the house, I would probably find her body there or in the attached bathroom. I tried to open the door, but it was blocked. I pushed my shoulder harder into the door, and it opened a foot or so until I could squeeze through. Inside, I stood on a great landslide of newspapers that covered the bed and floor two to three feet deep while stacked almost to the ceiling on the far side the room. Moving to the bed, I slid newspapers onto the floor, but found it empty. The master bathroom was also empty. I retraced my steps across the papers and stood near the bed, relieved that my partner would probably

YES, SIR! NO, SIR! NO EXCUSE, SIR!

find the body. It was then I noticed a movement near my foot. From beneath several feet of newspapers and without a sound, a withered, mummified hand reached for my boot. I believe my heart popped out of my mouth as I screamed and jumped away. Almost breathless, I called for my partner, and together we uncovered the tiny, emaciated woman buried beneath the avalanche of newspapers. Near death and terribly dehydrated, she was unable to speak and was taken by ambulance to the hospital. I never heard if she survived. Returning to patrol, my partner laughed as he said I screamed like a girl. I failed to see the humor.

THE MEDAL OF …

I hesitate to tell the next story from West Los Angeles Division, fearing that some might think me immodest. Like every cop, I dreamed of receiving the department's highest award for bravery, the Medal of Valor. While most were given for bravery during violent crimes, some were given for bravery while rescuing citizens trapped by fires. I was working the "J-Car" (juvenile detectives) on night watch. Near midnight, we were circling the blocks near the station, waiting for end of watch, when we smelled a particularly nasty burning odor. Following our noses to a street two blocks east of the station, we saw dark smoke billowing from the windows of a second-floor apartment. After calling dispatch for fire assistance and requesting backup, we jumped into action. My partner began alerting residents on the first floor while I pounded doors on the second floor. Coming to the involved apartment, I kicked the door open and entered into a choking brown cloud of superheated smoke emanating from the kitchen, backlit by a bright red glow. Gagging and stooping low under the smoke, I glimpsed a man lying on the sofa. Thinking he was unconscious, I crawled to the sofa and began to drag him to the door, but he resisted. Aroused from sleep and disoriented by the smoke, he apparently thought I was attacking him. I used pain compliance to get him out of the apartment to safety. Thankfully, no one was injured, and the fire department made quick work of "food on the stove." Their investigator determined that the man I had rescued had put a big pot of menudo on the stove and then fell fast asleep. Over several hours, the menudo had cooked away, and the steel pot and stovetop were red hot.

The sport coat, slacks, and shirt I wore had to be thrown away when several dry cleanings failed to remove the stench of burning menudo. After receiving a basic "atta-boy" commendation from my supervisor, I knew that no Medal of Valor was forthcoming. Several weeks later, I was unexpectedly called into the briefing room filled with division personnel where the lieutenant read a proclamation awarding me the "Medal of Menudo." Some say the laughter could be heard at the courthouse two blocks away. Needless to say, I was the subject of many menudo jokes in the weeks to come. As far as I know, I'm the only LAPD officer ever to receive the Medal of Menudo.

Many of the events I experienced, I could not process in a way that I could share with my wife. How do you remove pain, suffering, avarice, and brutality yet fairly convey the experiences of a policeman to someone who has never experienced the dark side of humanity? Sadly, I began laying the next level of the wall separating us as I compartmentalized my life. I could sense her confusion and frustration but felt helpless to do otherwise. My anger and grief from Southeast Asia had followed us to Las Vegas and Los Angeles, and I could feel the tension building in our marriage. I vainly tried to fill my growing emptiness with possessions, including a sports car, motorcycle, and camper, but the void was never satisfied by possessions. Life became a sinkhole devouring everything around me as it grew. Dreams of a happy life and marriage were fading, and I had no clue how to change course. When we spent holidays and vacations skiing or exploring the beauty of the West Coast, my mood changed for the better with every mile marker away from Los Angeles. Yet every time we returned, the stress and anger awaited. I searched in vain for other police jobs in Oregon and Northern California, but Los Angeles had us in its grasp.

CENTRAL DIVISION

Central Division was a truly depraved bouillabaisse of suffering and failure in the City of Angels. The privileged West Side now seemed a thousand miles away. The inner city vibrated with politics and commerce during the day but shrunk to a small, third world city of immigrants, derelicts, addicts, and predators after the evening rush hour as commuters fled to the safety of suburban living. Newly assigned officers were often assigned to the B-wagons, and I was no exception. I was tasked with transporting public drunks and prostitutes along skid row. After completing my first shift, I went home to my wife who was sipping a glass of wine while preparing dinner. Smiling, she came to me for a kiss. The wine on her breath triggered a flashback to the foul, overpowering bouquet of cheap wine and stench I had just left on skid row, making me nauseous. Needless to say, the pleasant dinner and evening she had planned evaporated.

How do you tell your wife that her breath reminds you of the hundred derelict drunks you handled that day? How do you tell her that your appetite vanished when you had to clean human vomit from your boots and urine soaked your leather gloves? How do you tell your wife you love her when you've crushed her spirit and can't eat her dinner? How does a cop love a woman? I had no one to ask, as there were no department chaplains or counselors, and my partners were divorced, some several times. I wrestled alone with my demons.

OFFICER NEEDS HELP …

After serving the requisite time in patrol, I was selected to work a felony car. This was a coveted position for cops who craved action. It was a plainclothes assignment in an unmarked car free from the tyranny of radio calls. You actively hunted predators, instead of simply responding after the fact to their residue. My partner and I had graduated from the academy together and were always able to anticipate each other's actions. During this assignment, work was fun and seldom boring. We led the division in felony arrests for months. One afternoon, nearing end of watch, I suggested we take our 1969, 440-cubic-inch Plymouth Police Special into the concrete channel of the Los Angeles River to play. The car performed like a rocket on the wet concrete, and we took turns burning rubber and skidding until we were both screaming with laughter. Behind the wheel, I decided to open it up and accelerated from beneath the Six Street bridge south toward Fourth Street. Speeding up river, we saw a group in the distance. As I slowed, they noticed our approach. At a separation of perhaps a hundred yards, I saw two flashes followed by a zinging past the open passenger window and gunshots echoing in the concrete channel. My partner screamed, "Shots fired!" and I stopped perhaps fifty yards from the group. He should have handled the radio, but after another gunshot narrowly missed, he charged from the car, leaving me to handle the radio.

"One Zebra 2, officer needs help, shots fired, in the LA River at Fourth Street ... in foot pursuit of multiple male suspects eastbound into the rail yard."

As I dropped the radio mike to follow my partner, I heard the dispatcher give a halting broadcast, "All units, officer needs help, Los Angeles and Fourth Streets. Shots fired. Unit available to handle?" Another unit quickly responded and thankfully rebroadcast the correct location. The suspects jumped the barbed wire atop of the channel embankment and quickly disappeared into the adjacent rail yard. Knowing that the cavalry was coming, I ran after my partner. I reached the foul river water at midchannel just as he cleared the fence atop the embankment and disappeared into the rail yard. Reaching the fence, I became entangled on the barbed wire, ripping my pants and drawing blood. I was angry at him for running into such danger alone, especially since we had no hand radio to communicate. In the rail yard, a switch engine slowly pulled a long string of cars, separating me from my partner. After several tense minutes, I located him several tracks away, and we systematically began to search the maze of open freight cars. The first air unit to arrive was a television helicopter whose low orbits made communication difficult on the ground. We tried to wave them away, but they merely waved back. With wailing sirens approaching from several directions, we knew that the Blue Crew would soon be on scene. After a thorough search of the rail yard, we arrested four suspects but found no gun. Walking them out to awaiting black and whites, I noticed that all four were bleeding from numerous barbed wire wounds. Apparently, they were no better at climbing a barbed-wire fence than I was. Other suspects had fled to the local projects where we would give special attention in the coming days. The watch commander cited us for our diligent police work, but he never asked, and we never offered, why we were in the river that day. Just another day of excellent police work for the people of Los Angeles, whose tax dollars had purchased some Plymouths with bad engines. The city turned down a claim for my boots ruined by the pollution of the Los Angeles River.

PLEASE, MR. PIG

On another summer day, we slowly drove the backstreets of skid row while discussing and solving the problems of Los Angeles and the world. The radio droned with a steady stream of calls reflecting a typical day in Los Angeles. Suddenly, the triple beeps preceding a "hot call" shook us into focus. "One Adam Four, handle a 211 (robbery) in progress at the Laundromat … Sixth Street. Suspect is a male Negro, black and brown, five ten to six feet. Suspect is wearing a bright blue jumpsuit and is armed with a handgun. One Adam Four handle code three." (Red lights and siren.)

I realized we were less than a block from the call and radioed, "One Zebra Two, code six on Sixth Street." In less than a minute, my partner pulled to the curb at the Laundromat. I exited the passenger door within ten feet of a man in a bright blue jumpsuit backing onto the sidewalk. My adrenaline surged. Officer survival training had taught that most shootings happen at very close range, and most shots miss due to adrenaline rush.

I screamed, "Freeze! Police! Don't move!" As I sighted my .38 on his broad back, he slowly turned toward me, and I continued shouting, "Freeze, put your hands up or I'll shoot you!"

He turned back toward the doorway, reaching toward his pocket. At that moment, a woman entered my peripheral vision from the adjacent doorway screaming, "Oh no, he's going to shoot Earl! The pig's going to shoot Earl! Oh Lordy, please, Mr. Pig, don't shoot him! Earl ain't done nothing." Her screams caused me to smile. It seemed like a slow-motion sitcom, only this was real life, and the potentially deadly encounter would be over within seconds. Squeezing the trigger, I watched the hammer coming back even with my eyes glued to the suspect waiting for the muzzle blast. In that moment, thoughts raced through my mind … "I'm really going to shoot him. The *LA Times* headlines tomorrow will scream: 'Witnesses say LAPD officer kills man while smiling. Officer indicted, career ruined.'"

Thankfully, Earl put his hands in the air and surrendered a millisecond before the hammer fell. I cuffed him and a quick pat down found a small knife that most carried on skid row but no handgun. It turned out that Earl had heard the victim's screams from his small business several doors down the street and ran over just after the robber had left. He was the second man wearing a bright blue jumpsuit to emerge from the Laundromat that day. We were looking for the first. I wrestled with the angry thoughts of what might have been. I switched to a foot beat on Main Street and came to intimately experience life from the perspective of society's underclass of prostitutes, pimps, addicts, parolees, homeless, and the hopeless. Their success on the streets was measured by daily survival and cheap highs seeking release from the pain of survival. It played out in low-rent hotels, grungy back alleys, needle-filled shooting galleries, and cheap lowlife bars. Lives were filled with black tar, grass, cheap whiskey, and cheaper wine. Here life was a daily struggle for those caught in its maze. My adrenaline-fueled experiences were always at someone's tragic expense as they were victimized by the brutal life and predators of skid row. An ancient, grizzled sergeant took me under his wing for several days as he demonstrated how to police effectively on a foot beat. He danced on the line between the brutality of street justice for criminals and gentle compassion for their often anonymous victims. I learned how to counsel resistant suspects in Central's numerous back alleys away from the bothersome glare of pubic scrutiny. It was rumored that he was the real-life Bumper Morgan immortalized in Joseph Wambaugh's novel, *The Blue Knight*. I know that I was glad that I wore the same badge and walked on his side of the line.

187 PC

Adrenaline serves to anesthetize normal emotional responses, and I found myself craving opportunities to numb the pain and the anger simmering within. I volunteered for a street crimes decoy unit in the worst area of Central Division. One afternoon, dressed as a derelict, I turned the corner at Sixth and Wall Street just as a large man carved open another man's chest and abdomen. I ran to the location where the victim lay mortally wounded. I radioed for backup and paramedics and went in foot pursuit of the suspect now a block away. My baton slipped into my right hand as I ran, and I was soon thankful for my decision to carry it that day concealed up the sleeve of my tattered jacket. As I closed on the suspect, I noticed that he was far larger than first appearance. Hearing his frantic breathing, I knew that I would soon catch him. When we closed, I grabbed his overcoat, and he spun to a stop, facing me with his hands up. It was a poor tactical decision for a supposedly wise street cop.

At that moment, a cop and a murder suspect stood at arm's length. I had learned to read suspect's eyes, and his seemed to say, "Okay, you caught me. I give up." Then, just as quickly, they flashed with the realization that he still held the bloody carving knife in hand only three feet from my face. His eyes flashed with the intent to kill another victim that day, but before he could move, I struck his right collarbone with my baton. The blow resonated like a bass drum through his large frame. His eyes rolled back, and he slumped to the ground unconscious, dropping the bloody butcher knife at my feet. Astonished, I quickly cuffed him and awaited backup. I never received a commendation for the arrest, nor did I ever go to court. It was just another day on skid row where life was cheap, and mine could have easily ended with careless tactics.

I could recount many such stories, but eventually the adrenaline rush wore off, and I could not fight the battles at home with gun or baton. During this period, the emotional wall between us continued to grow, and I pushed the one person who loved me away. In 1977, we purchased a new home in Thousand Oaks. It was exciting to have our first house, but it added the stress of a fifty-mile commute to work, and I quickly tired of the multitude of projects inherent in a new house. Instead of enjoying making the house our home, it became another source of conflict. Frustrated, I picked at my wife with sarcasm and anger. Emotionally wounded, she retreated, and our relationship grew distant. My dark nightmares continued, and life was gray, even in the bright Southern California sunshine.

FAILURE

One evening, I stood alone on the front sidewalk. Glancing down the street, I saw the row of new houses, shiny cars, and neighbors working in their yards. Turning, I saw our new house, a sports car, a camper, a motorcycle, and our golden retriever happily wagging her tail. Yet I was empty and alone. I thought I had found the American dream, but life was a sinkhole swallowing everything until I fell in.

My wife was inside cooking a meal that neither of us wanted or could finish without another argument. I gave into despair, and its darkness washed over me. Everything seemed broken in my life, and I had no clue where to turn or how to fix it. I walked into the kitchen. She asked if I was ready to eat, and without warning, I slumped to the floor sobbing. I had not cried since Bruce's death in 1969. The tears exploded from deep within, and a decade of anger, pain, fear, and grief flooded into our shiny new kitchen. I was broken beyond repair and could not speak. I refused her attempted consolation, and fear masked her pretty face. I believe it was the fear of watching someone you love slip away. The wall was now too high, and neither could cross it. I sobbed all night on the kitchen floor. In the morning, physically and emotionally exhausted, I drove aimlessly away. I left the one person who had committed to loving me "till death do us part." Something within had indeed died, and its moldering turned my life into a foul carcass over the next two years. Divorce seemed the only way out of the maze I had constructed, but I was unprepared for the utter sense of failure it brought. It was something that happened to others, to losers and quitters. So what did that make me?

We attempted reconciliation several times, but it wasn't to be. I have no blame for her. I always thought that she would take me back, but the day she said, "No more, I want a divorce," I was stunned. I now wonder why a woman stays with an angry man. She is the one splashed with the caustic effluent of misdirected rage. I wonder if she feared each day. I wonder if she blamed herself. I wonder if she wished she had never said, "I do." I wonder when she stopped loving me. Was it that night in the kitchen? Today, I know that she did nothing wrong. She was simply the casualty of "friendly fire," the misdirected rage that I had intended for myself. Immature, selfish, and angry, I was unable to love her. She was the second victim of my anger. I was the first.

Alone, my life continued gray and without purpose. The beauty and softness she had brought into my life was gone. I supplemented adrenaline rush with alcohol. Attempts at dating were shallow and engendered frustration and needless drama. Healthy women ran from me, and I ran from the others. As my social circle abandoned me, I joined a couple of miserable divorced cops, and together, we operated like a band of rogue male lions living outside of the pride. Unable to find acceptance, alcohol and shared misery became our norm.

A new nightmare began interrupting my sleep, and night after night, I awakened sweat-drenched and racked in fear. The dream always began in a grassy park on a sunny day. As I walked, I would slowly descend into a trench. I continued walking until the trench enveloped me and became so deep and dark that I could no longer see daylight. Fear coursed through me like molten lava, until I would awaken sweaty, shaken, and alone. My life at home and work was unraveling, and I was unable to stop it. I had lost my honor, and perhaps I never had control.

Driven by anger and desperation, I began driving into dangerous neighborhoods at night. I would park and aimlessly walk the dark streets. Within my jacket pocket, my right hand gripped a .38 revolver. I intended to shoot the first person that crossed me. I can't remember how many times I made that walk, but I was never accosted. Finally, exhausted and tortured, I turned my rage inward.

One night, alone in my cheap apartment, I stood before the bathroom mirror. I barely recognized the man I saw but knew I hated him. I cried out to God and placed the cold blue steel barrel in my mouth. The slightly sweet taste of steel, cleaning solvent, and gunpowder residue momentarily surprised me. Fingering the trigger, a force seemed to resist and paralyze my hand. The battle raged within for many minutes, but I could not pull the trigger. The promise of ending a decade of pain was so near, yet it danced just out of reach. I again cursed the man I saw, and salty tears mingled with the metallic taste. An interminable battle ensued, but I could not pull the trigger. My hand was frozen until I surrendered to a force I did not yet understand, perhaps the same force that had kept me from murder during those night walks in the ghetto. I staggered through another tortured night with little sleep.

My pain remained undiminished, and the failure of lost dreams grew. There were no answers yet. Would they ever come?

8

SEARCHING

I always assumed that I had the upper hand in our marriage and that my wife would forgive me no matter how harshly I acted. Following several halfhearted attempts at reconciliation, she looked me in the eyes and said, "I want a divorce. I can't take anymore."

Stunned, I saw no answer to the morass that had become my life. I had been promoted to detective after five years but found no relief from the unending pain. Work had become my morgue. Every day, another piece of me seemed to die as my life spiraled out of control. A detective lieutenant tried his best to salvage me, but I had lost interest in my career and in protecting and serving the people of Los Angeles.

In mid-1979, I took the elevator to Parker Center's fifth floor, walked to the personnel counter, and handed my detective badge, police ID card, and .38 revolver to the sergeant in charge. He seemed indifferent to my plight and made no effort to dissuade me from leaving. It was simply another meaningless transaction in his day. I signed a resignation form and walked out of my career as aimlessly as I had driven out of my marriage in 1977.

My life's compass fluctuated wildly without ability to find true north. I spent most of the next month lying on the beach trying to figure out life, but there was no "aha" moment. I tried pleading with God, but He remained as remote as he had while in college and during four years in the air force. I decided to visit the only people I felt I could trust. I flew to Clearwater, Florida, and settled into my parents' spare bedroom.

Mom's cooking tasted great, but there was unspoken tension in the air that even a tin of her oatmeal chocolate chip cookies couldn't cover. By the second evening meal, Mom tearfully addressed the elephant in the room. She was brokenhearted that I was divorcing, and they were grieving the loss of my wife whom they loved. I became defensive and took their comments as an attack. The meal quickly devolved into tears and recriminations, until I gave an ultimatum. If they continued to support her, they would lose me as their son. Mutually exhausted, we reached a truce and separated to lick our wounds.

My sister Sharon was living across the state near Miami, so I decided it would benefit all if I went for a visit. Her home was a welcome respite from the drama with my parents, and I enjoyed seeing her and my young nephew Jay. Fortuitously, I carried a copy of the alumni booklet I had received days before leaving California and discovered that one classmate, Bob Ritter, lived only a mile away from Sharon's house. Bob and I enjoyed a friendly phone conversation as if we had just seen each other a few weeks before. Now an airline pilot, he said that he was supposed to be flying that day, but something had prompted him to call off. He invited me over, and when I arrived, he suggested we go fishing. Before I could say no, we were launching his small outboard motor boat into Biscayne Bay. Churned by a strengthening wind, white caps lapped at the freeboard. My nervousness turned up a notch when Bob mentioned that a hurricane was a few days offshore and small craft warnings were in effect. He promised to stay close to shore.

Bob had flown F-4 fighters during the war, so I expected to share cold beer and greatly exaggerated war stories. We had shared many pitchers of beer while cadets in Charleston's cheap bars, but in his cooler, I found only sodas. We caught up on the decade past, including friends and classmates lost in Viet Nam. We sat facing each other in the small boat with knees almost touching and lines bobbing on the wind chop. Looking directly into my eyes, he smiled and said, "Bob, do you know Jesus Christ?"

As a cold shock flashed through my body, I remembered the story where Jesus walked on water, and for a brief minute, I considered the option. His bold question settled deeply into the empty void of my heart. I desperately wanted to respond, but fearful and unsure where it would lead, I explained why I had walked away from my faith as a teenager. I confessed that I wasn't a theologian, but I knew that if God was real, He wanted all to come and worship freely. I didn't understand why skin color was an issue in our church. I remembered singing in Sunday school that "… red and yellow, black, or white, they are precious in His sight, Jesus loves the little children of the world." I wanted no part of their hypocrisy and soon plied my parents with every excuse to miss church.

Cautiously, I began to ask Bob about God. Some were the unanswerable "why" questions that I used defensively, but at least a few were asked with sincerity. The spark inside I thought long dead seemed to ignite into a flame of truth as he shared how God had turned his life around and brought peace and joy into his life and marriage.

As the minutes passed, Bob asked, "Do you want to accept Jesus as Lord and Savior of your life? Can I pray with you to accept Christ?"

Deep within, I wanted to scream out "yes," but I surrendered to my fear and pride. I made a weak excuse that Bob graciously accepted. I promised to think further about our conversation, but I didn't tell him that it was burning in my heart. At dinner that night, I met his family, and I saw what I had been searching for since 1967. Their home was a place of peace and love, where Christ reigned. A day or so later, I visited another classmate. I was invited for dinner and experienced the same Christian love that Bob's home had radiated. I returned to Mom and Dad's where the truce held until I flew north to my sister Trish's home in the Maryland countryside. Far removed from city stresses, I found a wonderful refuge for several weeks. I especially enjoyed getting to know my young nephew Brett and even filled in as coach of his Little League team for a short time. On the return flight to California, the reality of failed dreams pressed in. I knew that I had not just disappointed my parents; shamefully, I had torn at the fabric of their love for me. Bob's recent conversation burned in my heart and jousted with guilt from the pain I had caused my ex-wife, parents, and friends. Painfully, I learned that divorce is never just about two people. I had important choices to make.

In California, I had met and casually dated Judy, the beautiful mother of two children, Sandra and Michael. We had met by chance through a counselor's bold attempt at kick-starting my life. Judy's sister, Kathy, and her firefighter husband, Greg, graciously opened their home to me in Huntington Beach upon my return from Florida. There I found the same peace, love, and faith that I had recently experienced in Florida. They never criticized me and seemed to genuinely love me. Many evenings, we sat and talked about their faith. Their answers to my questions burned with sincerity in my heart. Such love became irresistible, and I found myself being drawn toward a decision that would change the future course of my life. Now thirty-three, I had chased the American dream and found it to be a mirage of empty promise. It had cost me two careers, a marriage, and nearly my life.

Could these three examples of love be God's way of conversing with an immature, hardheaded, angry man? Jesus Christ was the common denominator in each example, and deep within I yearned for the peace and love that I had tasted in all three homes.

On September 21, 1979, I stood alone on a warm summer evening beneath a star-filled sky. I thought the night sky particularly beautiful, since beach haze and fog usually obscured the stars from view. With Angela and Ryan tucked into bed, Kathy busied herself inside with the unending tasks of a young mother. Gazing upward, I was suddenly overwhelmed by the sense of eternity that I had experienced as a young child. Something profound and holy was calling me, and for a moment, I thought I might collapse to the ground. It brought the clarity I had vainly sought for a decade. There would be no realization of the American dream without allowing the dream's author and architect to lead me. It was the most profound moment of my life, and my past paled in the present moment.

Taking a deep breath, I looked skyward and offered a short, desperate prayer acknowledging my sinfulness and need for a savior.

"Sir, I have no excuse, sir. I stand broken and sinful before you. Lord, I deserve nothing but your judgment for the mess I've made and the people I've hurt. Lord Jesus, please cleanse me of my many sins. Forgive me. I choose to follow You.

"P.S. Please don't make me go to church with all of those hypocrites."

Seemingly, I stood on the lip of the Grand Canyon about to take a step into its vast emptiness. Fear gripped me until I literally took a step and felt the firm concrete driveway under foot. Something magical yet very real had just occurred. Glancing skyward again, the stars seemed to dance in approval as if I had become part of a great celestial celebration. Simultaneously, a great burden was removed from my shoulders, and for the first time in my adult life, peace flooded into my soul! At age thirty-three, I met the irresistible force that had rescued me from my dark journey of self-destruction. I met the living God. He would now reconstruct the dream I had vainly pursued on my own. Hope replaced my despair. With Greg at work, I nervously sought Kathy to tell her of my decision, and she welcomed me into the family of God with a hug and joyful tears. The next morning, I could barely contain my excitement as I shared the good news with Greg. I wrote to Bob Ritter letting him know of my decision for Christ. Within days, I received back a letter of encouragement and celebration that I have treasured these many years. Bob remains a true friend and brother in Christ. He took me fishing and hooked me!

For a decade, my sleep was haunted with nightmares of anger, violence, and hatred that filled me with despair and left me exhausted. About a week after my decision for Christ, it seemed the nightmare had returned. Again walking into a trench, darkness enveloped me until suddenly I was lifted skyward by a fountain of pure white water out of the darkness and into brilliant light. When I stepped out of the water, I stepped firmly onto a rock. I awoke feeling cleansed and joyful. Imagine my surprise when a few days later, I read, "I waited patiently for the Lord and He turned to me, and heard my cry. He lifted me out of the slimy pit, out of the mud and mire, He set my feet on a rock, and gave me a firm place to stand. He put a new song in my mouth—a hymn of praise to our God, many will see and fear the Lord and put their trust in Him (Psalm 40:1–3 NIV)." It has been my life verse since that night when the nightmares stopped.

Even as God began renewing my life, I was still prone to make poor decisions. One such decision was to fly to the South Pacific by myself. Before accepting Christ, I had purchased a ticket to the islands to see if I could escape from the stresses that were weighing me down. In reality, I was going to run away from life. Traveling without the support of Christian friends, I was easy pickings for my old nature with all of its lusts and flaws. Christians call it "backsliding," and I did it with flair. I truly enjoyed seeing a beautiful part of the world, but I hated surrendering to my old nature. At one point, I fled western Australia to avoid an emotionally unbalanced woman looking for an American husband. When I spurned her advances, she menaced me with a butcher knife, hoping to change my mind. In full retreat, the decision to return home was made expeditiously.

Despite my P.S. prayer months earlier, I was soon attending church with Judy, Greg, and Kathy. God's word burned in my heart as He filled the void that the world could never fill. It seemed that every sermon preached and each song sung was just for me. It was a magical time of discovery and new life. While unemployed, I often sat up through the night excitedly devouring the Bible. The very book that once seemed dry and hard to fathom had been opened for me to revel in. It seemed that each author knew I was coming and was trying to feed me the wisdom of the ages. The following spring, I slipped beneath the salty waters of the Pacific Ocean and declared my faith in Christ by public baptism.

Greg and Kathy kept me in the nursery known as Uncle Bob's room for the next year. They never complained of my intrusion into their lives, and I will be eternally grateful for their demonstration of love toward me. During that year, Judy and I continued to date. She was attracted to me but remained cautious of the danger I represented with my old behaviors. Judy was determined not to repeat past mistakes and needed to see that my profession of faith was genuine before moving prematurely and endangering her children. Perhaps the best description of our dating was like walking on winter's first ice on a pond. It was attractive but tenuous, likely to crack underfoot, and best done carefully, if at all.

Old destructive behaviors seemed to evaporate. The anesthesia of alcohol became unnecessary, profanity left my vocabulary, and sudden fits of uncontrolled rage disappeared, replaced by newfound wisdom and grace. When I spoke of my faith and refused to join in destructive behaviors, old friends departed. New friends with kindred spirits soon emerged to cheer me on. My life became an artist's canvas with a new work being traced. The grayness of life evaporated, and each day dawned brightly with renewed hope and expectation.

The transition wasn't easy. There were still dark nights of battle for my soul, where the old nature fought desperately to reclaim what it once owned. I often felt like I was wrestling with the devil for title to my life. After ten years of marriage, I found it hard to believe that God desired me to be celibate. I devoured the scriptures looking for a loophole but found none. Rationalizing scripture, I surrendered to my old nature and found myself giving in to this compulsion with a woman I was dating. I was no match for her guile and weakly surrendered. After weeks of repeated behavior, I knew I was being disobedient and asked God for the strength to resist. One evening in a restaurant, I felt her toes play seductively with my calf under the table. She smiled coyly, knowing the dance had begun and I would surrender.

Without uttering a word, I desperately asked God for help, and He answered in a way that still amazes me. She spoke suggestively, and I countered with a statement of my desire to live as a Christian, and that we should abstain from further intimacy. She replied with several enticing suggestions for the evening, which I rejected. Suddenly, the seductive veneer was stripped away, and her rage poured forth. She became dark and vile, and I listened to her hatred for God and all things Christian. She angrily cursed God and ranted until diners in adjoining booths stared with annoyance. She demanded that I comply with her desires, but I knew instantly that the leash of sin had been severed. God's intervention showed me the ugly truth that lay behind the attractive and seductive covering of sin. I once again felt clean as I drove from her residence without looking back. I sang songs of praise to the God who hears and answers the prayers of His children, especially the deep cries of the soul.

I was soon convinced by scripture of my need to confess the sin of divorce and to seek forgiveness from my ex-wife. When I spoke to her about the amazing conversion in my life, it was greeted with the skepticism of a broken and emotionally abused heart. She was right to doubt me, and perhaps I expected too much. Before we parted for the last time, I handed her a new Bible with John 3:16 bookmarked, "For God so loved the world that he gave his one and only Son, that whoever believes in him shall not perish but have eternal life." It remains my hope that one day we will be united in God's family.

Judy and I now entered a new phase of committed dating and wrestled with the limits of God's grace. Did it extend to divorce and remarriage? Some Christians took the narrow view that such sin and remarriage could separate one from relationship with God. Yet, His word declared that with confession and repentance, nothing could separate you from His love. We committed to dating and loving as Christians. Some decisions during courtship were easy, others quite difficult. We were both scared to again face the agony of failure. Judy was an amazing woman filled with God's grace and wisdom, and dating became alive with the joy that had been missing from my life. She and her children were God's undeserved gift of love and made me complete in a way I had never before experienced.

Earlier years had been lived in shades of gray despair. Life now was a radiantly beautiful Technicolor, and life took on a new luster. A new chapter was beginning, filled with hope rather than dread. The decade-long carapace of anger was magically removed from my life. A new dream was being designed by the architect of dreams. It was being built upon a rock, and that rock was Jesus Christ.

9

SECOND CHANCES

Judy was a blend of Texas spice, beauty, and passion that I found irresistible. Our dating was full of adventures in and around Southern California that stimulated my zest for life and helped erase past failures and painful memories. We enjoyed beaches and ski slopes, museums, concerts, and church. Where I once lived frustrated, bored, and depressed, Judy awakened my heart to a new, positive framework for life. Perhaps best of all, we grew in our shared faith.

For a period, I supported myself by house painting with Greg. While his side job was honorable work, it was not steady and certainly not a career path. Judy adamantly insisted she would not consider marriage until I had full-time employment. I fired off resumes to a wide variety of businesses, certain that I was through with law enforcement. Rejection letters flooded back along with one solitary job offer. I promptly set that aside, since it was a law enforcement position. After months of futility, I reasoned about "the bird in the hand ..." and interviewed for a police position with a major railroad in Los Angeles. Within a few days, I was hired, and within a few weeks, Judy accepted my proposal of marriage.

On June 6, 1981, overwhelmed by her beauty and the reality of God's amazing grace, I almost fainted as she walked to me. Smiling, the pastor grasped my arm and steadied me while suggesting I try breathing. The vows before God and family were genuine this time and not merely lip service on my part. We enjoyed a quick three-day honeymoon in Laguna Beach, but work was waiting. Overnight, I was a new husband, stepfather, and railroad police officer. Our new family shrank to three when Michael decided to live nearby with his father during high school. His decision caused Judy great heartache, but she desired Michael's best before her own needs. Her depth of character was displayed, as it never would have been when life comes easy. Sandra also missed her brother greatly while simultaneously coping with a new stepfather in her life. Changes came quickly, and life was certainly not dull in our house. We purposed that our home would be a place of Christian love and safety for family and friends. "... But as for me and my household, we will serve The Lord" (Joshua 24:15b, NIV). We also agreed that divorce would never be an option for us. Judy's love for her children and friends gave me a model of grace rather than judgment. As a cop, I was trained to demand compliance. Now I was learning that love conquered a multitude of sin, and respect was best earned. Many days were a trip on a roller coaster, as testing came with rapidity. Far from perfect as a Christian, husband, or stepfather, I was determined to grow in my new roles. God joined us in lockstep as we marched into married life together without the optional parachute of divorce. I found that I could communicate my doubts, fears, and failures to her without condemnation or fear of rejection. There was no need to construct another wall of separation. At thirty-three, I was finally learning how to love God and to love a woman. The new test for my faith was learning to love teenagers.

Judy and I had won a weekend for two at a beautiful golf resort in the desert south of Palm Springs. It offered beautiful mountain and desert vistas and fine dining along with beautiful golf courses and spectacular grounds. On the first morning, we settled at a table overlooking the golf courses, ready to enjoy breakfast. Excusing myself, I went to the men's room to attend to business, when another man entered and stood next to me, similarly occupied. Giving a discreet glance, I realized that I stood next to my childhood hero, Johnny Unitas. As we washed hands, I said, "Johnny, I don't usually talk to strangers in the men's room, but the last time we saw one another and spoke, I was on a bus heading up Charles Street, and you were waiting at an intersection. I said, 'Hey, Johnny!' and you replied, 'Hey, kid. How are you?' 'Great, Johnny, great! Go Colts!'"

"So you're from Baltimore?"

"Sure am, but I live out here now."

We walked back together, and he took me to his table and introduced me to some great NFL quarterbacks who were staying at the resort for a golf tournament. When I took him over and introduced him to my all-star wife, he was truly gracious. I'll never forget enjoying a beautiful resort weekend with Judy and meeting one of my childhood heroes far from Baltimore. What a great memory.

Working as a railroad police officer, I now enjoyed statewide jurisdiction that enabled me to cross local and state political boundaries in performance of duties. Day or night, I could find myself driving throughout Southern California responding to calls for service. The majority of time was spent protecting the railroad's high-value freight and property from theft and trespassing. I rode trains and explored the web of rail yards, industries, and port facilities at will. It was refreshing working without the internal drama endemic within other agencies, and best of all, I was paid to play with trains. New automobile shipments were considered high-value cargo and were often the target of theft and vandalism. One evening, tasked with checking new automobile loads, I was only partially done when the train moved. I assumed it was being switched locally but was quite surprised when, about two hours later, I detrained forty miles to the east. I enjoyed a relaxing ride in the front seat of a new Cadillac with music playing on the FM radio. The lieutenant wasn't amused when he had to send another officer to retrieve me.

TUNNEL VISION

Another day, a train crew reported a possible dead body in the tunnel through the Santa Susana Mountains north of the Los Angeles basin. Railroad tunnels are dark and dangerous places at best. This one added running water and a mile of slippery, uneven footing to the equation. Joined by an operating officer, our flashlights barely illumined beyond our feet as we stepped carefully into the slippery darkness. Near the midway point, I asked my companion if the distant light was the far portal. At first unsure, he commented that the light appeared to be growing slightly larger. After a moment of nervous hesitation, we reached the conclusion that we were looking at the headlight of an approaching train. With nowhere to escape, we turned back and ran for our lives through the darkness. We reached the tunnel portal mere seconds ahead of the train and jumped to safety in the bushes. No human body was found in the tunnel that day, but we learned a valuable lesson about railroad safety that had almost cost two human lives. We soon emphatically shared that lesson with the train dispatcher who had allowed the train to proceed past a red signal.

LEARNING PATIENCE

The morning still of the yard office was interrupted by a commotion outside. Heading out the back door, I arrived just in time to prevent an altercation between the terminal superintendent and a union official. I separated them and sent the union official on his way until he cooled off. About a week later, the terminal superintendent called and expressed appreciation for my handling of the incident. He offered me the position of assistant train master in the operating department. It was a position that would immediately double my pay. After cursory prayer, I accepted the job and was soon supervision of trains and train crews in a local yard. I couldn't wait to call Dad to tell him, since he had labored for thirty long years on another railroad and had never achieved this position. He was pleased with my good fortune and wished me success in my new career path. I was flush with pride at my new accomplishment and good fortune.

The general manager summoned me with inquisitive interest. I was the first railroad policeman to make such a career move and knew I was under his microscope. This position was the first step in the career path to executive management and opened many new aspects of the industry to me. After several months of a steep learning curve, the honeymoon ended, and days off vanished. The new position began making demands on time and character that were troubling. Long work hours kept me from family dinners, midweek Bible studies, and time with Judy and Sandra. Daily conflicts with recalcitrant train crews and union officials often grew heated, and the fun of going to work evaporated. Angry behavior began to encroach at work, and I knew that I had made a major mistake.

One chilly night near the harbor, I stood alone in the rail yard, staring into the heavens, asking the question, "God, why did you allow me to take this job?" There was no answer from the night sky, but I did recall a scripture I had recently read. "Consider it pure joy my brothers and sisters whenever you face trials of many kinds because you know that the testing of your faith produces perseverance. Let perseverance finish its work so that you may be mature and complete, not lacking anything" (James 1:2–4, NIV). Reality was startling. I was blaming God for my own free-will choice. I had given lip service to prayer without the patience to await His answer before jumping into the new position. Through His word, I realized that my pride had led me to that place of misplaced blame. Asking forgiveness, I prayed for an open door according to His will and the patience to wait. He did so one year later while allowing me to grow in faith through additional tests that arose from my prideful choice.

One year later, I was offered a position with more normal hours but a significant cut in pay. After sincere prayer and with Judy's concurrence, I humbly took the position. The following week, the manager came to Los Angeles to greet me. He was puzzled that I had left the operations career path to take a position in claims with such a severe pay cut. I believe he really wanted to assess my sanity. Humbled, it presented an opportunity to speak to him of my faith. The year's experience in the operating department, coupled with my police and air force credentials, gave me credibility in my new position. Many coworkers sought my assistance when investigating accidents and injuries. I am certain I found favor because this time God had directed my steps. "In their hearts, humans plan their course, but the Lord establishes their steps" (Prov. 16:9, NIV).

NEW TESTS OF FAITH

God continued to use the workplace as a training ground for my faith. I had been in the claims position only a short time when I was called into the boss's office and told I would be laid off within two weeks due to budget shortfalls. He stared, expectantly ready to deflect an angry response. Instead, I calmly said, "God opened this door for me, so if it's closing, He must have something even better for me. We'll be fine, and I can't wait to see what God's going to do. He'll provide for us. I know it's not your fault this is happening." He appeared flabbergasted.

Judy and I prayed and praised God while wondering where this would lead. The two weeks went by quickly, and no layoff came.

A few weeks after the projected layoff date, I was again called into his office. Handing me back a recently submitted expense account, he asked me to increase the amount claimed and to resubmit it. I explained that the report was correct as submitted for about twelve dollars. He then ordered me to raise the amount by at least one hundred dollars. I knew I stood at the crossroads of faith and temptation with a profound choice to make. Money was tight, and I could have easily used another one hundred dollars a month. I reasoned that I could go along with the office practice and rationalize my sin or obey God's word and trust His promise to provide for His children. When I refused his request, he angrily demanded that I comply or there would be consequences. I explained that my Christian faith would not allow me to lie on the expense report. His red face and flustered demeanor reminded me of an air force general I had met a decade before. Several coworkers had eavesdropped and later cornered me in my office. They said that most people were padding expense accounts and that I would make them look bad if I didn't go along. I refused, saying that I sought to honor God by my conduct, causing some in the office to ostracize me. A few days later, the boss again summoned me. Entering his office, I expected to leave unemployed. I was stunned when he quietly apologized, saying that I had been right. He asked for my forgiveness and showed me the draft of a new policy for expense reporting. The policy rippled through the office, changing old practices to the displeasure of many coworkers.

GAINING FAVOR

Several weeks later, the business day started like so many others. My desk was covered by case folders that detailed accidents and injuries to employees. Once the investigation was completed, my role was to negotiate fair resolution to the employee's claims while also protecting the fiduciary interest of the company. I was often placed between the proverbial rock and a hard place, but I enjoyed the challenges inherent in the negotiations. Midmorning, a claimant entered the front reception area and asked for the deputy claims manager. Being busy, I thought little of it until I heard excited screaming and loud footsteps pounding up the hall. The assistant claims manager passed my door like an Olympic sprinter screaming, "Get out! He's got a bomb and a knife, and he's trying to kill me!" soon followed by the front door slamming closed.

The enraged employee followed with a butcher knife in one hand and a gas can in the other, screaming, " I've got a bomb. I'll kill you if you don't give me the money!"

Seconds later, as the receptionist's screams pierced the suite, I searched vainly for a weapon. Most of the claim's staff was out of the office, and the remaining staff fled quickly out the back door. Removing my coat and tie, I ran toward the receptionist's screams, expecting an imminent fight. She had been drenched with gasoline and threatened with immolation, but the attacker had vanished. It was eerily quiet as I guided her to a restroom, where I flushed her eyes with water while attempting to comfort her. When another employee entered, I asked them to evacuate to the lobby and to send the police. I found partial cover behind a wooden fire hose enclosure hanging on the hallway wall, giving me a clear view of the claims suite. A railroad police officer soon materialized at the far end of the marble-lined hallway perhaps seventy-five feet away. We had worked together and acknowledged each other while awaiting backup. Suddenly, the stillness was shattered when the office door flew open, and the assistant claims manager ran into the hallway screaming, "He's got a bomb! He's after me!"

Close behind, the claimant emerged and threw an attaché case, knocking him to the ground, followed by a loud explosion. With ears ringing and the smell of gunpowder, I thought there had been a bomb detonation. Stunned, my boss regained his feet and ran past me while the claimant disappeared back inside. When SWAT arrived, they found a barricaded hostage situation. The general claims agent (GCA) remained trapped in his office hogtied and drenched in gasoline. The suspect was demanding millions of dollars while threatening to set him afire and periodically beating him with a broken chair leg. After several hours of fruitless negotiations, SWAT finally entered and forcibly took him into custody. The attack traumatized all of the claim's staff, but we were ordered back to work without counseling or psychological support. The police investigation determined that there was no bomb. The loud explosion in the hallway was the railroad police officer discharging his .357 magnum at the suspect. The shot had narrowly missed the suspect, ricocheting twice off the marble walls, and finally penetrating the wooden fire hose case where I stood. The bullet was found inside the innermost hose loop, heart high. Weak kneed, I thanked God for protecting me from both an insane employee and from friendly fire. After that episode, I made sure to always have a defensive weapon handy in my office. The employee was sentenced to state prison, and I had the pleasure of officially denying his claim. Grumbling about expense accounts ceased, and peace reigned in the office. Some coworkers even praised me as a hero. I experienced the truth of "When the Lord takes pleasure in anyone's way, He causes their enemies to make peace with them" (Prov. 16:7, NIV). I mentioned to God that it would be fine with me if He chose less dramatic ways to give me favor with my coworkers.

HOW'S A BURGER SOUND?

I began a weekly lunchtime Bible study and invited all to come. Only two Catholic men responded. I suggested that we simply read and discuss God's word, avoiding discussions of doctrinal differences. Another coworker declined our invitation but made it his cause to ridicule and rudely disrupt our studies. Together we prayed for his soul, and together we grew in understanding. Our offices were located on the corner of Main Street and Sixth Street in the badly decayed commercial district where I had once walked a foot beat. Time and neglect had caused the once-famous transportation center for Los Angeles to transform into a relic shorn of its past opulence. I believe some of my coworkers invited me to lunch because they felt safer walking the mean streets with an ex-cop. Memories of police escapades arose wherever I went in the area. Several months after the attack at our office, my supervisor invited me to lunch. He was one of the two men who joined the Bible study but seemed burdened and given to frequent fits of anger over trivial issues. He reminded me of someone I once saw in a mirror. We sat close together in the back booth of the dingy burger joint at Seventh and Broadway, joined by the noon rush of street people looking for a cheap meal. There were more smells wafting about than just burgers that day. Tony and I initially shared little in common beyond the railroad, but he seemed drawn to me. He loved to hear police stories, but this day he was distant and burdened.

Tears rimmed his eyes as he said, "Bob, since the first day we met, I saw something different about you. I watched how you handled the expense account fiasco and the layoff threat with peace and dignity instead of anger. You were a hero when the crazy guy tried to kill everyone, yet you've been humble. I admire you. You seem at peace. What is it about you that's different?"

I flashed momentarily to another discussion in a small boat in Biscayne Bay just a few years before and replied, "The only good thing in me is Jesus Christ. I have lived much of my life without Him. I now choose to live with Him. Tony, if you see anything good in me, it's Jesus. Would you like to know Him?"

He tearfully spoke of the mounting anger and the frustrations in his life, and I gently shared the story of God's redemptive work in my life. Tony gave his heart to Christ that day in the cheap burger joint. Over the years, we became fast friends and celebrated our common faith in Christ until his death at Christmas, 2012. I know that he will join friends waiting to greet me when it's my turn to enter heaven. It's always good to have friends who know their way around wherever you go.

10

GOD'S WORD IS ALIVE

Then I heard the voice of the Lord saying, "Whom shall I send,
and who will go for us?" And I said, "Here am I! Send me."
—Isaiah 6:8, NIV

As a new Christian, I looked for opportunities to serve and grow in faith. For several years, I pursued Bible courses and was certified by several ministry schools. We were attending a nearby nondenominational church where we were warmly received and quickly brought into leadership. After serving as an elder for two years, I was asked by the pastor to fill the vacant assistant pastor's position. Sensing a call to serve God in ministry, I accepted with Judy's blessing.

Tony spearheaded a nice luncheon highlighting my humble beginning as a railroad policeman, promotion to assistant train master, claims agent, and now a pastor, all in several short years. I think many present scratched their heads in disbelief at my career path. Despite missing my coworkers and friends, I was excited to answer God's calling. I left the railroad on good terms, which would turn into a greater blessing than I could imagine.

Driving to church the next day, I pondered how an assistant pastor acted. I had no clue, so I figured I'd just continue to be "Bob." As weeks passed quickly into months, I became an encourager to some and a diaper changer to others. I came with the warts, blemishes, and directness that rankled the sensibilities of some. Thankfully, many liked me, but almost everyone loved Judy. It was her graceful support that helped me navigate my first attempt at full-time ministry. Church dynamics were challenging and far removed from my naïve expectations of spirit-filled consensus. In ministry, it's imperative to have the support of your marriage partner.

LEARNING THROUGH FAILURE

During the Christmas holidays, a friend graciously invited Judy and me to his mountain condo for the New Year's weekend. The sky was blue, and the crisp pine air was invigorating. As we settled in to watch the Rose Bowl, Judy decided to take a walk. Moments later, hearing her screams accompanied by the growls of a raging dog, I raced to the front door and was horrified to see Judy being attacked by a pit bull. By the time I turned and grabbed a fireplace poker, the dog had vanished, leaving Judy on the ground with a serious bite wound on her leg. After carrying her inside and calling paramedics, I began to search for the dog and its owner. A few houses away, I saw a scraggly-bearded young man working under the hood of a decrepit pickup truck. I approached, poker in hand in case the dog returned, and asked if he knew who owned a pit bull. He immediately became aggressive and charged into my face with curses and threats to get off his property. His foul breath reeked of alcohol and marijuana, and he pushed me backwards. Responding instinctually to his challenge, my c-clamp cut off his airway, and I raised him onto his tiptoes. White-hot anger flashed through me. As I raised the poker to strike him, a quiet voice pierced my rage and paralyzed my arm, saying simply, "I died for him too."

An electric shock coursed through me, and I involuntarily released my grip on his throat. He screamed renewed profanities and threats as he regained breath. Ashamed, I turned and walked back to Judy, convinced that God had intervened to keep me from destroying two lives. When law enforcement arrived, they arrested him on warrants, and his dog was impounded by animal control. Driving Judy to the ER, I quietly thanked God for saving me from my old destructive nature. Some lessons are learned through failure, and I had surely failed this test. Thankfully, Judy recovered without lasting injury, and we soon returned to our busy lives. I had so much to learn about walking in step with God and the extent of His grace.

THREE OF A KIND

Do not quench the Spirit … reject every kind of evil.
—1 Thessalonians 5:19 a, d, NIV

Two other younger men on staff also sought God's wisdom for the ministry. Over coffee, we discovered that we had each experienced the same dream that week in which a smoldering coal was breathed into flame. We joined in early morning prayer, seeking wisdom, renewal, and healing for the church and pastor. We hoped that the Spirit's renewing breath would blow through our lives and the church family. We were sure that God would move, and He did. We three were soon gone from the church.

OUCH!

It was on Easter morning when the IED went off. I was at church early, filled with excitement at the day's promise. Easter is the essence of Christianity, and it is the truth of resurrected life in Christ that separates our faith from all others. We have a risen Savior, the joyous answer to the dark challenge of Good Friday's cross. Sadly, a simple facilities conflict turned into a major disagreement, and I retreated to the refuge of my car. With mind racing, I tried to sort through the unexpected conflict. Questions flashed by without answers. Why do Christians act this way? Lord, how much must I tolerate? Wasn't I called to this ministry? Is my anger a sin? Am I wrong? How should I respond? Why? Sadly, at that moment the secular corporate world seemed far safer and easier to navigate. When Easter services started, I greeted our faithful, smiling through a wounded heart. I left church that day feeling betrayed and uncertain why God had allowed such behavior. I sought Judy's consolation and wisdom, knowing that my next decision would directly impact our family.

With her support, I quietly tendered my resignation. Needing to provide for our family, I swallowed my pride and called the railroad, expecting to hear, "Sorry, but …" Instead, my old boss immediately offered to rehire me, allowing me to start the next day. Walking into the office after a two-year absence, I was grateful for God's provision yet humiliated by self-perceived failure even as old friends warmly greeted me. I had entered ministry expecting Christians to both know and live out the scriptures with lives honoring God. It seemed that all too many were satisfied with simply knowing.

THE PERSISTENT VOICE

Young in faith, I struggled to process all that had happened and retreated into victimhood. Feeling spiritually abused, I was angry at God and felt guilty that I had brought pain and uncertainty into our home. Angry dreams once again stalked my sleep. I would awaken after each episode guilty and ashamed that I was desiring revenge and reverting to my old nature. I continued in that anger for months while keeping God at arm's length, trying to avoid further pain. I considered myself a failure despite Judy's loving support and encouragement.

The power mower roared loudly as I cut the front lawn on a warm summer day. Covered by the noise, I groused at God. I questioned why He had allowed two years of my life to be wasted. Hadn't I been called to ministry? Is this how You treat faithful men? My wife and friends had confirmed my calling. Were they all wrong? My tears of frustration tasted bitter that day as they mingled with perspiration.

Then through the mower's noise, a quiet voice asked, "Who persecuted my Son?" Startled, I looked around the cul-de-sac but saw no one on the street. I resumed mowing, until I heard the voice again, "Are you better than my Son?"

The questions pierced my heart, and I stood frozen in place on a hot summer day. I reasoned that it was the religious leaders who had plotted to persecute Jesus. Certainly, He had endured far more unjust persecution by religious leaders than I. Ashamed, I sat on the nearby wall and replied, "Lord, I know I am not better than your Son. I accept Your will for my life. Please forgive my anger and self-pity. I surrender again to Your will for my life."

Tears flowed, and with them, anger drained from my heart. I finished mowing while humming praise songs, and my tears were no longer bitter. The angry dreams ceased, and I again walked with the freedom and hope found through forgiveness. In a significant way, I had entered into a closer identity with Christ. Perhaps the two years hadn't been wasted. I had learned a valuable lesson through the pain.

Michael graduated from high school and began his long and distinguished career in law enforcement, followed soon by marriage to his beautiful bride, Carolyn. Now assigned patrol, Michael took me on a ride-along in a tough part of Los Angeles, and I saw his warrior's heart. The streets were meaner than I remembered, and I was thankful that he was much better trained than I had been. Judy and I have prayed for his safety for over thirty years.

Sandra blossomed into a beautiful young woman with an amazing zest for life. Her faith and beauty attracted many friends throughout high school and college. She was gifted in multiple sports, but above all she loved the Lord. Family life took on a new harmony as we grew together through God's testing. Another wonderful thing to come out of that experience was Wes, the young man who would become Sandra's husband. They met in the church college group, and he alone has proven to be well worth the pain of those two years.

A Fleece

I had barely settled into my old position when a new opportunity presented itself. The manager from another railroad called and offered me a substantial raise and promotion to work for him. Having gone eight years without a raise at a company hemorrhaging red ink, I jumped at the chance to ease financial pressures. The two railroads were as different as night and day. Where I once had waded confidently in shallow waters, I now dog-paddled in deep waters where expectations were high and competition was the accepted standard. Both companies were large railroads, but their management styles are best understood by contrasting a mom-and-pop grocery store to a big box store. One was comfortable and hemorrhaging profit margin, while the other was aggressively intentional about increasing market share and bottom-line profitability. After a few years in my new position, it became apparent that further promotion was unlikely, since those in management were all younger, and there seemed to be a clique of long-term managers firmly in control.

A FLEECE

The pager had an uncanny penchant for interrupting family events and holiday celebrations. I was growing tired of disrupted sleep and spending weekends and holidays in rail yards investigating accident scenes. Judy and I prayed, hoping that God would direct us, as He had Gideon. With nervous excitement, we decided that changing our future would mean "going big." We projected a move to the East Coast to begin our new life, and the fleece was our house. The housing market was soft in the mid-1990s, but we knew God would bring the buyer, or if not, we would have our answer. The realtor helped set a fair price, and we were flooded with prospective buyers, but no offers were tendered. After one month, the realtor suggested we lower the asking price, but we held fast. As the second month passed, he again approached, hoping to drop the price. Without having received an offer, we had received our answer. We took our house off the market, content that God wanted us to bloom where planted. We waited excitedly for what God had in store, and it was a short wait.

Within three months, the manager was terminated for personal failures that reflected poorly on the company following his criminal arrest. The vacant manager's position in Los Angeles was immediately advertised. A few days before the cut-off date, the vice president called and suggested I apply. Being the junior man in the office, I didn't think I stood a chance for the job, so I procrastinated. During a second call, she pointedly instructed me to apply. A week later, I was selected as the new manager for Southern California, which included four offices.

PETTY THREATS

The Lord is my light and my salvation, whom shall I fear.
—Psalm 27:1b, NIV

Prayerfully, Judy and I sought God's wisdom and protection in my new role. Soon, my new boss flew in to meet me. Snarling, his first words were, "You'd better know on which side your bread is buttered. You answer to me. Cross me, and I promise, I'll get you. I don't like you, I didn't choose you, and you'll never last as manager."

I was clearly not his choice for manager. Apparently, he intended to use any means necessary to see that I failed in my promotion. The following day, the claims staff attended a tri-railroad golf tournament. He told us to leave our company-furnished cell phones in the office but to carry our beepers. Giving into my get-even streak (probably the one Mom failed to spank out of me!), I arranged for a friend to use a local number to page him. It worked beautifully, and as he addressed his ball on the first tee, his pager sounded. When he realized that because of his edict, no one had a cell phone handy, he rushed back to the clubhouse. Rejoining us on the second green, he said that it had been a wild goose chase. As we were about to tee off on number three, his beeper sounded again. He stared at the three of us and threatened to fire us if we were messing with him. We stared innocently as he again headed to the clubhouse. Two holes later, a very flustered director stormed back to join us. As we made the turn to the back nine, his beeper sounded yet again with an 800 number from headquarters. He was convinced he was being played, but he couldn't risk not responding to a call from headquarters. When he departed in his cart, we laughed until we fell down. When he returned, he bristled with angry threats, but we remained mute. Both his day and golf game were shot. I engaged him with one other spur-of-the-moment prank a few weeks later, when he flew into LA and arrived at my office in a rental car that was the exact model and color of my company car. He was busy in the law department and apparently uninterested in dining with me, so I went to an early lunch. On a whim, I tried my key in his rental car, and it opened the door. My key also started the engine, so I quickly moved the car about fifty yards away in the same row, where I parked and locked it. When I returned from lunch, an angry director stood in the empty parking spot, swearing to a deputy sheriff that his car had been stolen. Despite my boss's certainty as to the exact spot where he had parked, the deputy insisted that they search the surrounding parking lots before reporting it stolen. After a brief search, they found the car. He was speechless as the deputy said that it was not unusual for out-of-town people to forget where they parked their rental cars. My boss had little to say the rest of the day, especially when I assured him I had handled similar calls when I was a cop. Apparently he didn't like the taste of crow.

Within two months, he too was gone from the company. His position was quickly advertised, and managers around the system eagerly applied. A few days before the cut-off date, the vice president called and instructed me to apply for the position. I demurred, saying that we desired to remain in Los Angeles because of family considerations. It would have been easier to skin a live bear than to separate Judy from our first granddaughter, Clarissa. On her second call, the vice president said the position was now being offered in Los Angeles. I got her drift.

A week later, I was the new regional director. My empire now stretched through all or part of ten western states. As God gave me wisdom and favor in my new role, many wondered at my rapid ascent. Moving for promotion was a ritual on the railroad akin to military service. In my twenty-four years working for two railroads in six positions, I never once had to move. Other railroaders were flabbergasted, as they came and went through Los Angeles with regularity.

I was now in deep water and had to acquire new strokes. I quickly learned that a successful director equips and empowers his employees to act. I watched with awe in the coming year as the western region became the standard of excellence. It had historically been the bottom dweller in performance among eight regions. I learned that it was as important to manage senior executives as it was employees. Where I had once been angrily confrontational with those in authority, I learned the art of assertive negotiation to the benefit of those who worked for me. The corporate world was a fertile ground to mature my faith, and I was tempted and tested on many occasions. To overcome the seductive new trappings of power and privilege, prayer became a constant companion in the competitive, secular workplace. My responsibilities in claims operations included management of accident and injury investigations, medical management of employee injuries, and claim resolution and settlement. I worked directly with the law department to defend the railroad in all noncriminal matters. Each phone call could be a simple question or an emergency call to respond to a major accident within my region. The challenging position was magnified since money was at the root of every action. Railroads were not under worker's compensation laws but rather an antiquated fault-based system called Federal Employer's Liability Act (FELA) that rewarded employee injuries and malingering with larger payouts. We were locked in a conflict-based system with litigation a very present threat. Regional payout was continually scrutinized by executive management since it directly affected bottom-line profitability and stock value. As the regional purse keeper, I was in a constant tug-of-war between competing interests that often became hostile. I attempted to maintain the difficult balance between legal fiduciary responsibility and fairness.

One year later, the two company's merged, and I was now the director for all of my old colleagues from the first railroad. It presented unique opportunities for all concerned and brought old friends back into my life.

I remain awed and blessed by how decisively God answered our prayers as a couple. Through our fleece, He demonstrated the patient love of a father for his children who need direction and encouragement to flourish. He also brought new ministry opportunities and broadened our dreams as husband and wife. We were blessed to maintain a cohesive family life with children and grandchildren despite corporate demands of time and travel.

A SECOND CALLING

A close friend from our prior church called unexpectedly and asked me to join him in starting a new church. Judy and I prayed again, seeking God's counsel. We agreed that I would join as a lay pastor and elder while continuing my corporate career. The new church was born and quickly grew beyond our expectations. It balanced the temporal, secular demands in my career with eternal values found only by exercising spiritual gifts. Church growth brought the need for additional pastoral care, and my friend's call to join him in full-time ministry continued on a regular basis. We struggled with our response. Were we resisting God's call?

In July 2001, with Greg's encouragement, I applied to and was selected by a large fire department to serve as one of their fire chaplains. It was the beginning of my spiritual calling to assist first responders and critical care victims. Having been a first responder and understanding firsthand the unique needs and pressures of police and fire careers, I hoped to make a difference for some who struggled with life, as I once did. I had no idea what lay in the near future.

SEPTEMBER 11, 2001

While driving to the office, breaking news reported a plane crash in New York. Paying little heed, I switched channels, hoping to find traffic reports to ease my commute. In the office, the first cup of coffee helped erase morning cobwebs as I prioritized the files and phone messages on my desk. It had promise of a busy day.

Moments later, my admin assistant entered wide-eyed and ordered me to turn on the television sitting on my credenza. Graphic images of destruction flooded from the screen, overwhelming us. Against a beautiful blue September sky, great towers belched smoke and flames. Thousands ran panic stricken from the scene as fire and police personnel rushed against the fleeing torrent into black clouds of choking dust and debris. News accounts were confused and contradictory as shaken reporters sought vainly for reason in the midst of chaos. News reports suddenly shifted to scenes of chaos in Washington where the Pentagon had been attacked while frantic rumors of additional hijacked planes raised fears of coordinated terrorism across our nation. My office filled with stunned employees seeking mutual comfort and support. Together we faced the reality of war with forces we did not yet understand. Our country was under attack, and like most in America, we were reeling.

As shock turned to anger at the unknown evil that had perpetrated this murderous act, I vainly sought a rational response. By evening, I hoped for a massive military response against whoever had perpetrated such ignominious acts of hatred. On Wednesday, the shock continued as graphic pictures of destruction and mayhem continued to bombard our senses. President Bush spoke from a pile of debris at Ground Zero, trying to bring calm and rationality to a stunned nation. Among his comments was a call for a National Day of Prayer and Remembrance on Friday, September 14. Our church joined tens of thousands of churches praying for the nation, but I felt called to something more. I wanted to serve God at Ground Zero.

THE PERSISTENT VOICE ... AGAIN

I heard the quiet voice as I backed from my driveway on September 14. "Make a house of prayer."

Brushing it off, I swung into traffic, already planning another busy day. When I turned into the office parking lot, it spoke again. "Make this a house of prayer."

I thought of the many tasks needing my attention before the weekend and again ignored the voice. The elevator ride was quiet, and I rationalized that I was far too busy to heed the voice. I had settled in at my desk with a cup of coffee when for the third time, I heard, "Make this a house of prayer."

Shaken, I realized that I was resisting the Spirit of God. Closing the office door, I prayed that God would forgive my disobedience and asked for the boldness to comply. I called two Christian friends and colleagues into the office and told them what I believed God was asking me to do. My invitation to join was met with doubtful looks and excuses. When they left, God's choice wandered in and sat down. He had recently given his heart to Christ in the very chair he now occupied in my office. He had been forgiven much and reminded me of myself some years before coming out of the muck and degradation of a worldly life. He was also the friend who years before had interrupted our lunchtime Bible studies. He was still rough around the collar and not yet church polished. I told him what I believed God was asking me to do, and without hesitation, he said, "Let's do it!"

A HOUSE OF PRAYER

The office complex was two large buildings joined by a common ground-floor atrium and four elevator banks. Each interior floor opened onto a balcony hallway overlooking the atrium with tables and fountain below. The glass atrium ceiling rising over six stories gave a cathedral-like appearance as sunlight filtered softly into the common area. God had good taste for His new house of prayer.

It was already past nine o'clock as we hurried to post simple invitations to the president's National Day of Prayer at noon. We had almost completed our task when the building manager tracked us down and forcefully asked who had authorized our postings and meeting. When I responded with "The president," she said she would not allow such activity without approval from the building owner who was not available. Reciting the president's call for prayer and the need for national healing, I threw myself on her mercy while promising to remove every notice immediately following the event. Finally, her demeanor softened, and she relented. She too was shaken by the events on September 11.

Back at my desk, I grumbled halfheartedly that no one would respond on such short notice. Just before noon, two of us went to the atrium lobby and waited nervously. Some people hurried past, ignoring us, intent on their lunch breaks or running errands. Silently, I asked God to bring His people while selfishly hoping to avoid embarrassment. My admin assistant joined us, and now three waited. At noon, the bank of elevators began to cycle busily between floors. A few joined us, but more rushed past into the parking lots. As I asked those gathered to join in prayer for our nation, staff from a congressional office brought their American and state flags into the atrium. Suddenly, a torrent of people flooded from the elevators, almost filling the area. Toward the rear of the throng, I caught a brief glimpse of my two friends standing near the building manager. After greeting the crowd, I offered a short prayer of intercession for our nation, its leaders, and the families devastated by the terrorism of September 11. When I stopped, a woman's voice cried to God, followed by dozens of voices, one by one blending into a chorus of prayer flowing into heaven's hall. When finished, over a hundred people lingered in the area, united in spirit and reluctant to leave. There were tears, hugs, and words of appreciation from many people, once strangers, now united by prayer. The exhilaration of obedience was tempered by the shame of having resisted God's persistent voice.

I began removing the notices when a voice behind me asked what I was doing. Turning, I saw an expensively suited man and explained that I had promised to remove the prayer notices immediately following the gathering. Assertively, he said, "Leave them up." I repeated my promise to the building manager to remove them, and he replied, "The building manager works for me. I own these buildings. I like them. Please leave them up as a reminder for us all to pray for our nation." He handed me a business card and, shaking my hand, asked, "What else can I do for you? How can I help you?"

Thanking him, I promised to be in touch if there was further need. As we parted, I glanced at the card and recognized the name of one of the richest and most powerful men in California. At his request, the congressman's staff left their flags in the atrium as a memorial to honor the nation's dead.

Alone, I took the elevator to my office, marveling at a God who moves the hearts of men without partiality. I sat quietly at my desk reflecting on what had transpired. I wondered why I so often doubted

God and was thankful that I had finally obeyed His persistent voice. Indeed, He had provided a new Christian, who had not yet learned to doubt, to assist and encourage me. A few minutes later, two friends walked in and closed the door. Meekly, they asked my forgiveness for not having helped. Both said they had never seen a clearer moving of God's Spirit, and I agreed. All three of us had shared a measure of doubt, but our tears and smiles seemed fitting on the day Jehovah Raphah, the God of Healing, called for a house of business to become a house of prayer. The healing had begun, but great new tests of faith awaited.

The Fire

Like everyone, I was transfixed by the horror that terrorized America. On September 11, 2001 and the days following, television was filled with horrible images of devastation and grief on a scale beyond comprehension. Shocked reporters vainly babbled in the aftermath, trying to gain a toehold of reason. Wounded survivors emerged like ghostly apparitions from great clouds of smoke and ash, desperately seeking safe refuge, where three thousand innocents lay buried in the rubble. I wanted to turn away from the images, but like most others, I was drawn into the terror. I felt personally attacked, and as I wrestled with empathy for the lost and their grieving families, a deep-seated anger was demanding vengeance. I prayed fervently, but anger blossomed in my heart. Select personnel from our fire department responded to Ground Zero to assist in rescue efforts. When President Bush addressed the nation from the pile of debris, I felt a deep calling to serve but found every official door closed. At church and work, I led prayer vigils for the victims' families and nation while wrestling with an ever-growing anger toward the Islamic terrorists. My Christian faith was tested once more by the anger rising unexpectedly from my old nature. Would it once again rule my life and cause another decade of personal ruin?

On a blustery early October night, a fast-moving storm system filled the sky with towering clouds and showers scudding quickly on the west wind. The moon and stars occasionally danced between the billows and lit the night sky with beauty. As we exited the freeway en route home from church, I mentioned to Judy that one towering cloud to the east resembled the smoke header from a fire. Indeed, it was the fire that would prepare my heart to serve at Ground Zero.

Early the following morning while making coffee, I heard my fire pager beep forlornly from my jacket pocket. Dispatch advised that I was needed at a fatal house fire. I responded quickly to a scene of utter devastation. What had once been a typical two-story suburban house was now a pile of smoking rubble. News cameras sought the best angles for the morning broadcasts and interviews from anyone they thought could provide fact or conjecture on the tragedy. Already on scene, another chaplain briefed me on the terrible circumstances before us. Once home to a family of five, only the injured mother survived. A dad and his three young sons remained entombed in the smoldering debris. Firefighters stood in small groups, dazed and exhausted from their vain efforts to rescue the father and sons while also protecting neighboring houses from the raging flames. Chaplains soon learn that caring presence often speaks louder than words. We began to circulate among them, hoping our quiet presence would mitigate at least some of their pain and sense of failure. Later, we moved into the knots of close-knit neighbors on the street who were visibly shaken. Grief was palpable on both sides of the yellow police tape, and the shared grief of the community was overwhelming. Extended family members arrived and stared in disbelief, too stunned to respond to overtures of assistance. Shaken city officials deflected attention from the family as they grieved. Finally, arson investigators led a team in body recovery from the smoldering rubble. All four were found curled together in an upstairs bedroom under the collapsed roof, where a young father had attempted to rescue and protect his sons. The fire captain on the first arriving engine wept openly in frustration as his crew helped carry four body bags into the backyard. A short while later, I was asked to join the recovery team in the backyard where, shielded from news' cameras, the deputy coroner completed his investigation. Resisting a wave of nausea, I quietly asked God to allow me to comfort those grieving this catastrophic loss, especially the mother. I was joined by a Catholic priest who arrived to perform last rites. The father was a practicing Catholic, while the mother and sons attended a local Protestant church. Together, we anointed the four body bags and prayed for God to receive their souls with the mercy and grace found only through Jesus Christ.

We spent the rest of the day comforting neighbors and fire personnel until we were both exhausted. Later in the week, I was asked by the mother to speak at a memorial service. As I prepared comments, I wrestled with God, asking, "Why?" I received His answer as I read Hebrews 12:28–29, NIV. "Therefore, since we are receiving a kingdom that cannot be shaken, let us be thankful and so worship God acceptably with reverence and awe for our God is a consuming fire." I realized that God doesn't need shaken, angry servants. He needs willing servants filled with awe who will be agents of His comfort to the suffering. When I spoke at the memorial service, I was filled with wonder at such a God who received this burnt offering and noticed that anger no longer stalked my thoughts. The mother recovered and continued to serve as a teaching assistant at her children's elementary school to honor their memory. She also rebuilt the house. Such faith! I found that neither the fiery trial of September 11 nor this tragic fire would shake the kingdom of God. Humbled, I was being prepared by God to serve on His behalf. He was still on the throne!

THE FIRST TRIP

The hotel had only been reopened for a few days after being damaged by the towers' collapse. It sat a short block from Ground Zero, and we had only to gaze out a window to see the devastation that extended for blocks. The recirculated air had the lingering odors of jet fuel and chemicals, but the hotel offered a warm bed and shower. Our church team served twelve-hour shifts around the clock. We were based at the northeast corner of Ground Zero in the basement of St. Peter's Catholic Church. It was the church where victim #0001, FDNY Fire Chaplain Mychael Judge, was laid to rest on the altar, following his recovery from the debris of the North Tower on September 11. It was the refuge for many angry, filthy, frustrated, and exhausted rescue workers. Our role was to care for the physical, spiritual, and emotional needs of these men and women. The needs were legion.

An acrid odor permeated Lower Manhattan unlike anything I had ever smelled or tasted. It was a potpourri of burnt metals, cement, chemicals, plastics, and toxic jet fuel intermingled with death that hung heavy in the dusty air. We constantly wet-mopped the care center to reduce the dusty toxins tracked in by rescue workers, but it was a losing battle. Many of the recovery crews appreciated our care and invited us to tour the pit to see the site for ourselves. The scale of the pit was immense. Several subway cars were still in the pit after being recovered from the tunnel station under the towers' site. From the rim, they appeared as matchbox toys. Sadly, they had yielded bodies during the recovery effort. The debris had also yielded the amazing "Ground Zero Cross" found on September 13 during rescue efforts. It was placed on the Church Street side of the pit as a symbol of hope to all. The cross was a visible reminder that God is present through the worst of times.

The team jury-rigged a coffee cart and began a nightly trip around the recovery perimeter to meet, feed, and encourage the cold, lonely police sentinels stationed for blocks in all directions. Within a few days, many of our new police friends came to share the comfort of hot food and the emotional support we offered during their rest breaks. Everyone who entered had a personal story of loss, some overwhelming. One retired firefighter vainly searched for his firefighter son for over two months, sleeping for a few hours on a wooden pew. His son was never recovered. The week passed quickly, and before we knew it, it was time to return to California. Before leaving for the airport, an FDNY chief unexpectedly presented me with a Ground Zero Service Medal, in memory of service to the fallen. I wear it to this day on my fire chaplain uniform to honor the brave men and women who rushed through great choking clouds into harm's way.

With new friends imprinted on our hearts, we believed that we had made a small difference by sharing God's grace and provision to wounded souls. As we flew west, the call to return burned in my heart. I began planning a second trip with a new team. It was early December when we received the call to serve at Ground Zero once again. We were to serve at the same rest center, and we eagerly flew east.

THE SECOND TRIP

Rescue teams were now officially recovery teams as hope for rescue of the living passed. The exhausting regimen of dirty, morbid work accompanied by constant funerals had pushed many past the breaking point. Both fire and police departments were forced to cycle suburban crews in to replace the crews who had labored without rest for two months. Strangely, some of the newly arrived crews seemed to resent the duty. Winter brought additional misery to the site with snow and sleet, and depression hung like a heavy curtain around Ground Zero. The first night, I offered hot coffee to several firefighters who had just entered the church basement from the wet night. We made small talk, and they asked where I was from. I advised that the team of volunteers was from California, and they were astonished. They thought they were carrying on alone and that outside help had abandoned them after the initial September response. They celebrated us as "heroes" for coming so far, until I put a firm stop to such nonsense.

PEANUT BUTTER FAITH

The second day, we were told that the rest center would be closing due to a shortage of food and drink. Discouraged, I wondered why God had allowed us to fly across the country to hear such news. Supplies were down to cookies and coffee, and many of the recovery crews began looking elsewhere for hot food. I sat apart with my negative thoughts until a team member suggested we ask God for food to keep the center open. As we gathered to pray, I wrestled with pastoral guilt for not having taken the initiative to pray before surrendering to worry and disappointment. After praying, we pooled our money, and with about twenty-six dollars, one couple walked to a nearby deli where they were able to buy several loaves of bread and jars of peanut butter and jelly. We were determined to serve the exhausted teams, but our meager supply of sandwiches was quickly eaten. A few hours later, we sat together in the nearly empty room with hope quickly fading when the church door opened. A man entered and asked if we could use two hundred hot meals twice a day for a week. Astounded, we helped unload catering carts sent by a major restaurant in New York filled with delicious hot meals. God's provider returned faithfully twice a day for a week, and our first responders were well fed and well blessed. That same afternoon, another man entered and offered a truckload of soft drinks and water that would last the week. As we unloaded the truck, we rejoiced together, grateful to serve an amazing God who opens closed doors and multiplies fish and loaves, or in this case peanut butter and jelly. Who says miracles were only for biblical times? God, help my unbelief.

FEAR OF FLYING

Following the "aimless walk" described in the prologue, the week went quickly, and I once again found myself at Newark Airport preparing to fly home. Drained physically and emotionally, I booked a seat away from my team, hoping to enjoy a quiet flight. I began to relax in an aisle seat when the middle seat remained empty. As the flight attendants prepared the plane for takeoff, the woman seated by the window unexpectedly grabbed my right arm and sobbed, "I'm afraid to fly. I don't know if I can do this. Please help me!"

I quietly prayed, *Lord, I'm exhausted. I have nothing left to give. If you want me to help her, then please help me!*

As we taxied, I reassured her about airline safety and that I would be there for her to talk to if she needed. She explained that she was going to care for her dying aunt in California. With her permission, I said a quiet prayer that seemed to calm her. After takeoff, she asked why I had been in Newark, so I briefly described our team's service at Ground Zero. Through more tears, she voiced guilt that she lived in nearby New Jersey and had not been able to assist at Ground Zero. She asked for details of our service and wondered if God would ever use her in such a way. I gently suggested that her trip to love and comfort her dying aunt was both heroic and significant, and that God would be with her on this journey. I gave her an FDNY pin I'd received from a fire fighter at Ground Zero, and she promised to wear it and pray for those serving. As the flight continued, I gently asked about her faith. She spoke of her belief in God and occasionally attending church, but she didn't understand a personal relationship with Christ. A short time later, she prayed to receive Christ and cried tears of joy. I experienced a dichotomy of joy and shame. Joy that I had been used by God to bring her to salvation, and shame that I had selfishly wanted a quiet flight. God demonstrated that He always has work to do and that He was just beginning at my point of exhaustion. What an awesome ending to an amazing week.

These reflections, along with hundreds more from Ground Zero, resonate in my heart to this day. They have forever changed how I look at the world, relate to others, and attempt to live out my faith.

13

WHY ME, LORD?

In early 2003, Judy announced her well-earned retirement. To celebrate, we planned a two-week Maui vacation along with children and grandchildren in late June. Life was busy and exciting, and we all eagerly anticipated the vacation, until a phone call endangered our plans.

I was seeing a dermatologist regularly for many youthful indiscretions in the sun. After many negative biopsies and treatments, two additional biopsies gave me little cause for concern. Several weeks passed when the doctor called and asked if Judy and I could come into the office the next day. I thought it unusual, since it usually took weeks to get an appointment. The following day, we sat in a small exam room opposite the doctor and his nurse. He spoke with medical directness, "Mr. George, you have an aggressive malignant melanoma with nerve impingement in your right hand, and you have squamous cell carcinoma by your left eye. Sorry it took so long to contact you, but I wanted my diagnosis confirmed. You need surgery as soon as possible. After I get clear margins, I would like to refer you to the best melanoma surgeon in the United States for further care. It's where I would go if I was in your situation."

Stunned, I seemed to detach and float to the upper corner of the room where I looked down on four people. The doctor spoke to Judy and someone who looked like me, but little registered. After a few minutes, the four stood and shook hands. Outside, numb and weak, we collapsed on a bench. When I asked Judy what he had said, she replied that I had an aggressive melanoma and needed immediate surgery. She prayed while I cried.

A few days later, the doctor referred me for a more invasive surgery involving both the tumor and lymph system. My previously strong faith wavered, and I dissolved into tears as fear looked me squarely in the eyes, and I blinked. We retreated to our home trying to make sense of it. " Lord, why me? I'm a pastor and a fire chaplain! I'm the one who cares for others! Why now? What about our vacation plans? Lord, I'm doing so much for you. How can this be?" I cried daily in the shower, using that privacy to grieve, bargain, and argue with God. I even began to plan my memorial service. It was quite a pity party. Through it all, Judy was my rock of support. Although she was battling painful neck injuries from a recent car accident, she postponed her own cervical surgery to care for me. Together, we finally caught our breath and turned with faith to face the future. Judy prayerfully reassured me that I would be healed. With faith rebounding, I reasoned that God wasn't surprised and had allowed cancer to enter my life. He was more than willing to take the journey with me. Instead of "Why me?" I began to ask myself, "Why not me? Would it be better if someone else were afflicted?" I wasn't thrilled by the sudden life-changing event, but I knew many were praying for me. Finally, I found God's peace in the storm.

I chose to take the vacation. The second surgery was scheduled for the week following our return from Maui. It would be at a national center of excellence for melanoma surgery.

We had a great vacation despite some physical challenges and injuries. Michael had to drive me to the hospital the first night when I suffered severe anaphylactic shock from a prescription medication. Finding emergency medical care at night was an adventure.

On the phone:

Michael: "Can you tell me how to get to the hospital?"

Operator: "Well, drive back through town to the airport road. Follow that through the cane fields to the processing plant and turn left. Take that road to an abandoned drive-through and turn right. You'll pass more cane fields. Follow that for a while, and turn right at the fork in the road near several large trees and a white house. Follow that road past the airport sign and continue to Wailuku Road. After a while, you should see a sign directing you here. It's on the opposite side of the island."

Michael persevered through the dark cane fields, and following emergency treatment, I was able to breathe again, and the swelling and hives began to slowly subside. It was an auspicious beginning to our family adventure, but we persevered and together enjoyed the beauty of Maui. It was great tonic for our battered souls. We also discovered the beautiful music of IZ, which seemed to be playing in every restaurant and shop. His soft Hawaiian ukulele ballads became part of my emotional healing following surgery.

I returned home to a chaotic railroad. While in Maui, there had been a catastrophic train derailment in Los Angeles. My staff was overwhelmed by the needs of displaced families, so two of my peers rotated from their regions to cover my position. When senior management realized that I remained unavailable due to my pending surgery, they were displeased. It would lead to another unexpected turning point in my life journey.

Within days, I lay wrapped in warm hospital blankets against the constant chill, waiting for the early morning trip to the operating room. Judy's loving presence and prayers brought me sweet comfort. The hospital chaplain entered and asked, "How can I help you this morning?"

I replied, "Please go, find more people, and come pray for me."

He did, and they did.

Recovery was a painful adventure. There were serious side effects from the nuclear medicine used to trace my lymphatic system, and I had to be catheterized for several weeks. That added greatly to the post-surgical pain and slowed my recovery. After one very painful misadventure when the doorbell rang, I learned to exercise caution when standing up to avoid stepping on the catheter line (Ouch!). I also discovered that cancer affects both soul and body, and recovery must happen in both realms.

My faith deepened as God walked with me through the painful journey of self-discovery and healing. The simple beauties of life were enhanced, and I loved to sit in the warm California sunshine watching the world continue to function around me. My physical senses awakened as I enjoyed the enhanced beauty of creation. I matured into a deeper appreciation for God's presence in the midst of both blessings and trials. I was learning empathy.

Our family, church, and the fire department were wonderfully supportive. We were overwhelmed by the outpouring of love. Little did I know that God would soon use this as the springboard to my next chapter in life, a second opportunity at full-time ministry.

14

REFINING THE CALL

Following recuperation, I returned to work at the railroad, but my heart was again being pulled toward ministry. The church we helped establish several years before needed a second full-time pastor. Corporate life with its redundant conflict and travel became boring and often made me unavailable to serve both at church and as a fire chaplain. After repeated entreaties from the pastor and elders, we decided to take the plunge. In 2004, I notified the railroad of my early retirement and began round two of full-time church ministry.

The next several years were filled with a variety of ministry opportunities within the church. I enjoyed teaching classes, filling the pulpit when needed, and assisting the senior pastor in several ministries, but my heart yearned for more. I found myself better suited to lead volunteer teams in service to the community and its first responders. Following a wild lands training exercise in Southern California's fire-prone hills, we barbecued lunch for a battalion of exhausted firefighters. Enjoying the scene, the battalion chief warmly thanked me and said that this was the first time that anyone had ever reached out to them with such caring service. He continued that typically the engine companies would leave for their stations dirty, tired, and hungry immediately upon the conclusion of training. We watched together as the church team fed and engaged them with such hospitality that no one left early. Returning to church, the team was exhilarated from the experience.

Later that year, we did the same for a battalion of 450 young marines about to depart Camp Pendleton for Iraq. The average age of these warriors was about nineteen. We provided a beach barbecue for the marines and their dependents, along with live music. I happily greeted and thanked each marine and dependent waiting in the food line, until my surgically repaired hand was throbbing. I silently prayed for their safety, hoping they would return to the blessings so many take for granted in America. As the last young marine filled his plate, the battalion commander joined me. He was a battle-tested officer, perhaps ten years younger than myself. His chest was covered by ribbons, including both the Silver Star and Bronze Star for valor and a Purple Heart. His viselike handshake almost caused me to yell, "Uncle."

As tears filled his eyes, he said, "Thank you for loving my marines. I watched you speak with and touch every one of them in line. They're about to go into battle, and some may die. They need all the love they can get. During my career, I've never had anyone love my marines like that. Thank you."

Humbled, embarrassed at how little I had done, and now fighting my own tears, I managed to choke out, "It was my team that did it. We all loved on them, Colonel … (pause) … By the way, where are you from?"

"I'm from Baltimore," he replied.

"I knew it! Me too! Let me buy another Baltimore boy a burger."

We enjoyed lunch, reminiscing about our younger, more innocent years in Baltimore. All too soon, he returned to the deadly serious work of readying young warriors for battle. Returning to church, our volunteers were once again exhilarated by their sense of fulfilled ministry. Such fulfillment often takes place outside of church walls, as Christ's love is poured out to the lost and suffering. We discovered that love is an action verb seldom fulfilled sitting in a church pew.

KATRINA

In late August 2005, a great wind roared into the Gulf of Mexico and intensified into the monster storm we know as Katrina. With huge tidal surge and winds about 170 mph, it overwhelmed the levees protecting New Orleans and caused hundreds of thousands of residents to flee. Beachfront communities across East Texas, Louisiana, Mississippi, and

Alabama were devastated. The federal government mobilized USAR teams (urban search and rescue) across the nation, including one from our local fire department in Southern California. As they left on the dangerous and exhausting rescue mission, my chaplain's heart and prayers went with them. I asked church members to join me in providing humanitarian aid in the disaster area, and one volunteer stepped forward. A police chaplain joined us as we filled the church pickup and mobile kitchen with food and water and headed east, just three days after Katrina ravaged the Gulf Coast. After a hot, grueling drive across the desert southwest, we rolled into El Paso close to midnight where a sympathetic fire department graciously shared their beds and kitchen with three weary strangers. We slept with the firefighters in a large, open bay where we were awakened on multiple occasions by automatic room lights and a woman's soft voice.

"Engine seven, medic seven, truck ten assist the police, Taser victim at ..." Despite repeated alarms throughout the night, our tired bodies soon fell into blessed sleep. We departed in the early morning with coffee, sandwiches, and good wishes supplied by our new friends. After a second hot, tiring drive across the vast open spaces of West Texas, we made it into San Antonio. I no longer recall who, but someone from church had contacted friends, who again showered three unexpected guests with Texas hospitality. The third day, we pressed on to Louisiana. Before leaving California, I had arranged to meet the owner of Shields of Strength (Reg) along the freeway in East Texas. I had purchased military style dog tags from his website to give to police, fire, and military during ministry outreach in California. Driving over from Beaumont and refusing payment, he graciously donated five hundred dog tags with an American flag on one side and Joshua 1:9 (paraphrased) on the other: "I will be strong and courageous. I will not be terrified or discouraged; for the Lord my God is with me wherever I go." They would prove to be an invaluable morale boost and Christian witness in the weeks to come. Later, I heard that his home in east Texas had been damaged by the hurricane, but he came to encourage and support our ministry. His Shields of Strength ministry continues to thrive and blesses many people across the United States.

At almost every gas and rest stop across Texas, travelers inquired about our journey and often graciously paid for our gas and food. Others donated cash and added six new chainsaws to our overloaded truck and trailer. Another kindhearted man fleeing with his family advised that gas stations in Louisiana were unable to pump gas due to power outages. He purchased and filled ten five-gallon gas cans for us to carry into Louisiana. We were continually amazed and blessed by the spontaneous outpouring of love from American hearts.

Entering Louisiana, road conditions deteriorated as the interstate crossed a vast width of swamplands and bayous on uneven, elevated concrete sections, which caused us to crawl along at about twenty-five mph to avoid trailer sway, bucking, and nausea. Prior to slowing, the trailer had bottomed out as we pitched over the first jointed sections. When we arrived in Kenner, the western suburb of New Orleans, flooding and wind damage surrounded us. The city appeared deserted except on the far west side where a family offered us shelter for the night. The next day, along with several pastors from local churches and a Red Cross representative, we met with the Mayor of New Orleans' representative who declined our assistance, even as a massive rescue mission continued in the city's flooded districts. As dozens of helicopters flew overhead, fire, police, and Coast Guard boats plied the dirty floodwaters searching for stranded survivors. We passed several long caravans of buses headed west. In concert with FEMA, local officials had decided to send survivors to encampments across Texas rather than care for them locally.

The city lay inundated in a chaotic struggle for survival. In many neighborhoods, houses were marked in bright paint by rescue teams to avoid duplicate searches as the flood waters receded. In muddy fields, hundreds of automobiles, fishing boats, and pleasure boats lay piled haphazardly wherever receding floodwaters left them stranded. Dozens of coffins washed into a neighborhood surrounding the city's oldest cemetery. Katrina had transformed much of New Orleans into an eerie ghost town. We ended the day by assisting our host in cleaning out his flood-damaged office suite. Mold was already forming from the heat, humidity, and toxic water. As a precaution, we donned masks and gloves, washing salvaged items in bleach solution to kill the mold.

The next day, we headed north across Lake Pontchartrain's twenty-eight-mile causeway. Traffic was restricted to a single lane in each direction, since the parallel causeway remained closed by storm damage. As we lost sight of land, wind-whipped waves crashed against the rocks protecting the causeway, throwing spray over our truck and trailer. Gladly leaving the turbulent lake behind, we found a rest center for first responders in St. Tammany Parish. While there, we discovered the rigid, metal propane line running underneath the trailer had been ruptured and pushed through the floor, narrowly missing gasoline cans and supplies stored inside. It apparently happened on the rough stretch of highway entering Louisiana, and we thanked God that there was no fire or explosion. The local hardware store was closed by storm damage but gladly opened for firefighters seeking parts to repair the gas line. They improved trailer safety by designing a removable flex line while traveling.

St. Tammany Parish had dodged the storm's worst and was on the way to a return of basic services. They suggested that the city of Bogalusa, further inland, still needed assistance.

DARK WATERS

Bogalusa, with a population of approximately fifteen thousand, was originally a sawmill town founded by the Goodyear family in the early 1900s, surrounded by vast forests close to the Mississippi border. Decades later, a large paper mill and chemical factory replaced the sawmill, which had once been the largest in the world, producing over one million board feet of lumber a day. The city is situated on and named for the dark, lazy, tannin-stained river called Bogue Lusa, meaning "dark waters," by the Choctaw Indians who once called the area home.

The trip over a storm-battered two-lane highway into the northeastern "toe" of Louisiana was an eye-opening experience. Hurricane force winds had spawned dozens of tornados in this area, and we passed through apocalyptic scenes of destruction for miles. Great swathes of trees and hundreds of power poles lay snapped, broken, twisted, and uprooted. Many intruded perilously over the highway, forcing careful navigation through, under, and around downed branches and wires. Abandoned homes lay crushed and broken by the great trees that once provided cooling shade. Those still standing stood as barren sentinels denuded of leaves and Spanish moss by Katrina's fury. Nearing town, we passed through empty, battered neighborhoods whose residents had fled the hurricane's fury. Most of these refugees would soon return to broken, chaotic lives. City streets were restricted to first responders who had tirelessly manned chainsaws, desperately seeking access to neighborhoods in their search for survivors. Passing through National Guard checkpoints, we were directed to the police station in the heart of the city. The city had also endured several nights of looting by desperate survivors who remained in the now tightly controlled city. Communications remained dark in the parish, and help from state and national resources remained unavailable even as rescue helicopters and planes droned continually overhead en route to New Orleans.

LOCAL HEROES

In police headquarters, we met the first of many local heroes sitting in a small office, exhausted from his efforts to care for the community's and first responder's spiritual well-being in the days following Katrina. Overwhelmed by our unexpected arrival, his bear hugs and tears welcomed three strangers as the answer to fervent prayers. He immediately arranged for a police escort through the community to orient us to the scope of need. In one neighborhood, a mother and her preteen daughter sat on the front porch steps holding each other while rocking and weeping. Their modest house lay crushed by a large tree. Following the storm, they remained on the porch, sharing only two small bottles of water and a granola bar. Weakened and emotional, she said they had prayed for three days waiting for help. Openly crying, she asked, "Why didn't God answer our prayers?"

I replied, "I know He heard your prayers. Three days ago, God sent us from California. It just took us three days to get here. Please, we have food and water for you, and the doctor would like to help you if you have need." Later that day, we were able to assist them with shelter and further care. There were literally hundreds of similar needs throughout the community among those who had not evacuated ahead off the storm's fury. Watching many of these people who had lost homes and possessions respond with faith and gratitude toward our meager care was both humbling and convicting.

That evening, we situated the trailer on a grass lot behind the police station and jail complex and began providing light meals to first responders, city employees, and local jail prisoners. The chaplain provided anything needed with a quick phone call to a city official or a local businessman. He seemed to know and love everyone, and it was reciprocated during this time of emergency. National Guardsmen recently returned from a combat tour in Iraq maintained twenty-four-hour checkpoints throughout the community and kept order and rationing at the city's lone working gas station. SWAT officers from Birmingham, AL, enforced the dusk-to-dawn curfew while also caring for the poor with provisions of food and water, since local store shelves were empty. Police and fire agencies from across the nation arrived to relieve local officers exhausted from days of heroic rescue efforts. Volunteer paramedics and nurses supplemented exhausted hospital staff and manned triage centers caring for the sick and injured.

We planned to sleep in the field adjacent to the trailer, but one new friend called a local motel owner who opened rooms for us without charge even though the motel was closed by storm damage. It was truly a blessing after sixteen-hour days of nonstop activity to fall asleep in a cool, clean bed away from the heat and large, voracious mosquitos blown north from the swamps around New Orleans. The owner refused our offers of reimbursement, so we blessed his housekeeping staff with salary they would have lost had the motel remained closed.

ANGOLA

Three inmate trustees from Angola Prison, generally considered among the most dangerous prisons in America, were detailed to cook and assist us. The first breakfast, we served oatmeal, granola bars, hot cakes, eggs, coffee, and a few other basics that didn't seem to excite the southern palate. Fortunately, along with the trustees came a truckload of Louisiana sausage and large cartons of cheese grits sent by a local business lacking power to run its refrigeration. By the third breakfast, rescue personnel smiled and lingered over hot bowls of cheese grits and spicy, Cajun Andouille sausage. Supervisors had to pry them away to return to field duty. Many asked for and received the same meal for lunch, greatly simplifying meal planning. We were suddenly as popular as a new burger joint giving free double-doubles, even among the city jail inmates who ate far better than normal. Between meals, we had opportunity to speak informally with the trustees. Two were serving life terms for murder, and a young gang member from California, twenty-five to life for attempted murder, robbery, and drug sales. They were detailed to us after years of good behavior at Angola. Working long hours alongside one another soon broke barriers and fostered a level of trust even for this old cop. Later that week, led by our police chaplain, two gave their lives to Christ. Who could have expected such a blessing in the midst of chaos?

With a police escort, we provided daily outreach into isolated neighborhoods still lacking basic services. A doctor from San Diego and a nurse from the local hospital joined in providing home health care to many isolated seniors suffering from long-term illness. Their smiles and hugs were payment in full.

I WILL BE STRONG

On September 10, I walked over to the fire department across from the police station, hoping to visit with the on-duty shift. One of the chief officers stood alone behind the station, staring into the distance. He had earlier avoided my overtures as chaplain, even while giving me access to his exhausted crews. I approached and saw he was crying. I paused to silently pray for him and then approached and stood quietly beside him. He sobbed quietly for several minutes. I assumed he was suffering from the exhaustion and anxiety caused by Katrina. Finally he spoke in a halting whisper, "I wish I could have saved them. I should have done more to protect them … but they didn't tell us what it was … I didn't know … they didn't tell us …"

Confused, I asked him if he had lost firefighters in the rescue effort following Katrina. He replied, "No, ten years ago, the chemical plant had a large fire and toxic chemical release. I was a captain, and my men were exposed to the chemical cloud. We weren't told what it was and didn't wear masks. After a few years, they started getting sick. I should have done more. I should have protected them better. It still haunts me."

The anguish and exhaustion from Katrina had apparently triggered a delayed PTSD (post-traumatic stress) episode. Guilt-ridden, he blamed himself a decade later for the firefighters' injuries from the toxic fire. I asked if we could pray, and he nodded. Finishing, I gently told him of the guilt, anger, and blame that defiled my life for a decade and the peace I had found in Christ. After a few minutes, he sighed and asked if I would lead a 9/11 memorial service for his department. The following day, I was privileged to conduct a simple memorial service commemorating the fallen first responders from the terror attacks on September 11, 2001. As I spoke to the gathering of fire, police, guardsmen, I was overcome with emotion at the realization that I was surrounded by men and women with the same brave hearts that I had met at Ground Zero. I was in the presence of heroes, and I loved them. Following the short service, I retreated behind the fire station, thanking God while trying to process all that had taken place. A hand touched my shoulder, and I turned. Smiling, the chief officer handed me a Bogalusa Fire Department shirt, saying, "Thank you. You helped me yesterday, and my men today. I wish I had more to offer you."

We stood quietly and watched the sun dip into the haze covering the city of "dark waters." In such times, even small graces matter. Later, we shared some very tasty spaghetti and spicy Cajun sausage prepared by the trustees. Of course, I spilled sauce on the Bogalusa Fire Department shirt, which I proudly wore.

The fabric and character of America is stitched together by such heroes. They may have different accents and skin tones, but all have the same heart. Hundreds of heroes in Bogalusa received a dog tag reminding them, "I will be strong and courageous. I will not be terrified or discouraged; for the Lord my God is with me wherever I go" (Joshua1:9 paraphrased). I could leave them in no better hands.

As we packed the trailer to depart the following morning, the Birmingham SWAT team invited our small team to the gym where they were quartered, where they surprised us with a delicious dinner of barbecued steaks, baked potatoes, and salad as thanks for our service to them. We learned that you can't outdo southern hospitality even during difficult times. Try as we might, we couldn't get the cops to tell where they found the steaks in a city with empty store shelves. The memories of new friends and our shared experiences helped pass the long drive home, and I knew I would soon return.

A REPRISE

I spent two weeks at home catching some much-needed rest while preparing for a return trip. After sharing photos and ministry testimony at church, I again asked for volunteers, and six men responded. Two of us would drive the truck and trailer while the others flew east. At the New Orleans airport, we rendezvoused and headed for Bogalusa. It was a happy homecoming as we renewed friendships and surprised the prison trustees who were unaware of our return. New team members were welcomed with southern hospitality and love. We formed two teams to assist in downed tree removal from residences, utilizing our recently donated chainsaws. Local officials directed our assistance to the most needy families. God graciously spared one of our team members from serious injury when his chain saw suddenly snagged on a hidden wire and kicked back across his chest. The ER staff cared for him well and cautioned that they were treating more chainsaw injuries than anything else during the emergency. Great strides were now being made in returning Bogalusa to a semblance of normalcy. After a few days, the mayor asked us to come by his office, where he surprised us with a City Proclamation followed by newspaper interview and photos. It seems that newfound celebrity was competing with the call to ministry. Although thankful, we were there to serve others not to be celebrated.

The next day, a relief team from California unexpectedly stopped at our rest center en route to Bay St. Louis, Mississippi. After renewing acquaintances over cool sweet tea, they invited us to join them in Bay St. Louis. The small gulf town had suffered a direct hit by Katrina and was now laid ruin. With Bogalusa recovering, it appeared that God was opening a new door. Drawn by a desire to serve where most needed, we prepared to leave our friends but not before I was asked to speak at their local church. The midweek service was standing-room-only as several Bogalusa churches joined in a service of thanksgiving. I spoke briefly from 1 John 3:18 (NIV), " Dear children, let us not love with words or speech, but with actions and in truth," followed by a PowerPoint slideshow memorializing our time spent with them. When the lights were turned on, tears abounded. Church members shared their heartfelt gratitude that we had come from California to assist them in the midst of their need. Seeing themselves, local first responders, and friends in pictures detailing the breadth of destruction had begun the deep healing of their wounded hearts. Local churches, once bound by strict, traditional boundaries, were being renewed in common faith, and we knew that they would reciprocate if ever needed. The potluck following the service was filled with dishes prepared from generations of southern culinary expertise. It was a wonderful mix of southern hospitality and Christian love. One filled the stomach; the other filled the heart. It was difficult to leave such friends.

AN OPEN DOOR

Bay St. Louis, Mississippi, was an old southern beach town where stately mansions had once graced the bay front like a strand of expensive pearls. As we drove along the beach road, only their stone front steps remained, mimicking memorial stones in a cemetery. Katrina's tidal surge had pushed houses, furnishings, cars, boats, and trees into great heaps of debris perhaps a quarter mile inland. The small downtown area lay devastated. Where a bank once stood, only a concrete reinforced steel vault remained. I believed the sincerity of numerous hand-scrawled signs warning of "Danger! Black Mold!" and "Looters will be shot!" posted on the few remaining storefronts along forlornly empty streets.

135

Near the high school, we found a large sports field turned into the relief center. It sported several large circus-style tents offering shade and respite from the unrelenting sun and humid heat. To one side were sleeping trailers, showers, and chilled food-storage facilities. A tent town for displaced families and volunteers blossomed to the rear. Near the front entrance were the kitchen and dining areas. We quickly plugged into their well-organized relief effort and assisted wherever needed.

Survivors received food, shelter, clothing, financial aid, and even roofing repair donated by Christian volunteers from across the United States. The unofficial state flags of Louisiana and Mississippi became the blue tarps covering thousands of roofless homes from further rain damage. Pilots reported the blue pattern extended for hundreds of miles across Katrina's path of destruction. To meet spiritual and emotional needs, church services, pastoral counseling, and sporting activities were offered for children and adults, hoping to return a small bit of normalcy to residents caught in crisis. Local authorities relied heavily on this ministry effort to assist in recovery. Eventually, the center morphed into a new church, which continues to bless the people of Bay St. Louis.

I spent several days as chaplain trying to encourage exhausted fire fighters and police officers both spiritually and with financial aid. They were provided trailer homes brought into the area by FEMA so they could continue serving the community. At their request, I provided a belated 9/11 memorial service echoing the sentiments I had shared in Bogalusa. Each first responder and family member received a dog tag, reminding them, "I will be strong and courageous. I will not be terrified or discouraged; for the Lord my God is with me wherever I go" (Joshua 1:9 paraphrased). Every day, police cars and fire engines from a myriad of states would pull into the rest center asking, "Do you know where the chaplain with the dog tags is? Can we get some for our families and the guys back home too?" It began as a simple idea in a godly Texan's heart, yet it blessed many in the midst of suffering. They were indeed Shields of Strength.

All too soon, it was time for our team to depart, and we again headed for California. In a little over a month and a half, I had driven almost ten thousand miles and worried that the truck seat might need to be surgically removed when I reached home.

Arriving home, I reflected on the distinctions and similarities between the ministries at Katrina and Ground Zero. One scene had been the result of pure evil in the hearts of men, the other by great forces of nature. One had been confined to a relatively small site within America's greatest city. The other destroyed indiscriminately across four states. Though dissimilar in scope and cause, the survivors' needs were the same at both. At each disaster, amazingly brave-hearted first responders served to the point of exhaustion and responded selflessly. At both, we joined an army of Christian ministries from across the United States seeking to provide the critical needs of food, shelter, and medical care while also helping grieving hearts find the beginning of healing through God's grace. Man's hatred and nature's fury ripped at the American fabric, yet at both, I witnessed faith renewed and hope returning to wounded survivors. At both, I saw souls saved and welcomed into God's family. Isn't that the magical way of God!

Chaplaincy at both disasters was physically and emotionally exhausting but a blessing beyond measure. It was a privilege to have been used by God, and many wonderful memories remain from service at these two great American tragedies.

"And let us not become weary in doing good, for at the proper time we will reap a harvest if we do not give up. Therefore as we have opportunity, let us do good to all people …" (Galatians 6:9–10a NIV).

FINALLY ... CLARITY

Returning to California, I needed a time of rest and recuperation for my tired body. A period of restricted ministry activity seemed to hint once again at coming change as the emphasis on chaplaincy and critical care ministry waned. A few days before Thanksgiving, Judy and I prayerfully left the church we had loved and nurtured. Although deeply saddened, we purposed to seek God's direction even while facing an uncertain holiday season.

Standing alone in the yard, I praised God and thanked Him for our blessings, even as He had turned left when I expected to go straight. I felt a sense of wonderment at His sovereign purpose, which far surpassed my understanding even as the heavens surpassed my vision.

I spoke quietly. "Lord, I wonder what You're going to do with a man still four years away from retirement age. Since it's holiday time and no one is hiring, I can't wait to see how You're going to provide for us, especially for an old guy like me. We trust that You have a plan and are excited to see where You will lead us. So, Lord, this one's on You. Lead on!"

A few days later in a red vest and temp job, I assisted customers buying big screen TVs during the pre-Christmas rush in a local big box store. Proving the Peter Principle, I had reached my level of incompetence. We still viewed an old television with rabbit ears, and I knew little about plasma, LEDs, or LCDs. I was further humbled by surprised neighbors who were shopping unaware of my recent change in employment. Lifting big screens, cold concrete floors, and a bad back were a poor mix for a sixty-one-year-old without health insurance, so I encouraged God to please hurry!

Following a chaplain callout, I found myself drifting through the fire department headquarters. The assistant chief hailed me into his office. "Bob, I heard that you have left your church. Is that true?"

"Yes, sir, it's true."

"Do you have any plans for work?"

"Well, I'm working part-time, but we're trusting God to provide beyond that."

"Would you consider working here?"

"Sir?"

"There's an admin job open. What kind of computer skills do you have?"

"Well, I've had some basic software training, but I'm certainly not skilled."

"It's your call, but I think you'd do fine. Why don't you go talk to them?"

"Today?"

"Sure, I'll call and tell them you're coming down."

"Wow, thank you, Chief! If they hire me, I promise I won't let you down."

He replied, "I'd never have offered if I thought you might."

After several interviews, I was offered the position. Although it was full-time with benefits, it wasn't a permanent position and could be discontinued each year. Providentially, it lasted four years and allowed me to reach railroad retirement age. Judy and I were ecstatic. Less than two months after asking God to provide, He did, and a new ministry awaited.

The first day, the department head briefed me on expectations. She understood that I continued serving as a chaplain for the department but said that I could not act as a chaplain during work hours. When I agreed, she turned me over to a supervisor who quickly found dozens of tasks for me. It was a sharp learning curve, but it was interesting, and I enjoyed each day. The offices were new, equipment first rate, yet some coworkers were unsure why a chaplain was now working with them. It was an interesting and challenging first week.

The department head and her deputy were waiting at my desk when I arrived early on the following Monday morning. They ushered me into a small conference room, and I thought that my career was ending as quickly as it began.

She said, "Bob, we need a chaplain."

Surprised, I replied, "Excuse me?"

"We need a chaplain."

"Okay, I'll call one for you."

"No, we need you … now!"

"Excuse me? But we had agreed that I couldn't act as a chaplain during work hours."

"That's over. We need you. One of our employees died last night, and people are upset. I've called an all-hands meeting in a half hour, and I want you to speak."

"Excuse me? You want me to speak?"

"Yes, come on …"

That quickly, God redefined my call to ministry. I was a fire chaplain, not a local church pastor, and I was thrust into service helping a hundred shocked and grieving employees cope with their friend's unexpected death. I'd like to say that I had profound and moving words that day, but beyond sharing Psalm 23, I cannot recall what I said. I do know that God gave me favor with many, and in the coming weeks and months, they would seek me out to ask the "Why?" questions or to pray with them in the file room. Others asked me to lunch, so we could have deeper conversations, and friendships began to take root. Soon, employees in various headquarters departments who had never had access to a chaplain began to seek me out. God allowed my chaplaincy to flourish. I found myself continually thanking God for leading and providing for us so richly. I was now serving full-time in my calling, not just to firefighters but to all fire department personnel. It was a position God had uniquely equipped me for and very different from pastoral ministry. It became startlingly clear how the pain and disillusionment of war and military service, my experiences and failure as a cop, a divorce, two pastoral ministries, a corporate career, crisis training as a chaplain, and even cancer were all part of preparing me for this calling. God's gift set for chaplaincy is distinctly different from pastoral ministry. Chaplaincy is a ministry of presence, often in the midst of crisis. It brings hope to the suffering, calm in the midst of chaos, and encouragement to the struggling. A chaplain extends the hand of empathy and, when appropriate, a hug to console the grieving. I now understand that chaplaincy is a high and holy calling to serve those in the grip of their greatest fears and suffering. Through pain and failure, God had sculpted my heart of stone into a heart of compassion for the suffering.

In several chapters, I have recounted life-changing experiences as a fire chaplain. There have been times of joy at weddings, prayers and celebrations at academy graduations, and well-earned retirement ceremonies but far more times comforting the brokenhearted at memorial services and interceding for the suffering at accident scenes or in emergency rooms. Several experiences stand out as illustrations of chaplaincy.

SUCH FAITH!

There have been calls almost too great to endure. Thankfully, Judy and fellow fire chaplains who understand have always helped me persevere. One afternoon, I stood between two beds in a trauma center. A grandmother and her adult daughter were being treated for injuries suffered when a speeding truck had rear-ended their car on the freeway en route home from a happy outing to Disneyland. Tragically, the mother's three young children had died on impact. Paramedics, fire fighters, and police officers on scene were traumatized, and several chaplains were called out to assist them. I was detailed to the trauma center where hospital personnel were guarded in response to the mother's insistent questioning on the children's condition. After sedatives were administered, a CHP officer asked me to join him as he made the death notifications. His grim work completed, he retreated from the room, leaving me alone at bedside to endure the anguished screams of denial and primal, heartbroken grief from a mother and grandmother who had just lost three precious children. I could not speak. I simply held their hands and cried with them. As the sedatives calmed the immediacy of their pain, a man rushed frantically into the room, shouting, "Where are my grandkids? Where are the babies? How are they? No one will tell me."

Before I could answer, his wife screamed out, "Our babies are dead. They're all gone, every one. We've lost our grandbabies!" and a renewed chorus of grief erupted from their shattered hearts.

When he approached, he crushed me in a bear hug and dragged me to the floor. His body heaved as he shouted angry denials and screamed his grief in my ear. I doubted my capacity to bear such pain. I don't think I could endure losing one grandchild, much less all of them. I found no words to match his depth of loss. We lay there ... two strangers locked together in grief ... crying. Finally, I excused myself and allowed them time to grieve privately. Outside, I spoke with the shaken firefighters and paramedics who lingered, seeking comfort in community. After several numbing hours, I went home exhausted. Judy held me, and we cried as I recounted the tragedy.

Their memorial service was beautiful, and the family displayed God's peace and grace as they spoke of their three angels. I marveled at their faith. Several years later, I read a wonderful tribute in the paper telling how the parents had adopted several children to rebuild their family. Such love! Such faith!

BARGAINING WITH GOD

One morning, I was called to a hospital where a seven-year-old redhead lay on life support. He had drowned in the bathtub following a seizure while his mother was in the nearby bedroom getting ready for work. Approaching him in the ER, I was reminded of my grandson. Hospital staff and his devastated mother and grandmother all stared tearfully at me, looking for comfort. "May I pray with you?" I asked. We encircled the unconscious boy, and, holding hands, I prayed fervently for his healing, asking God for a miracle, desperately hoping the boy would awaken.

A short time later, he was transferred to a children's hospital in gravely critical condition. Before leaving, the emergency room doctor took me aside and said he would not survive if taken off the ventilator. Following the ambulance, I bargained with God and begged Him to save the boy, taking me instead by exchanging my breath for his. Apparently, God thought that was a poor deal, because He didn't answer my entreaty. At the second hospital, his mother, overcome with guilt and fear, explained that her ex-husband would blame her for the accident. She said he had treated her with explosive anger since their divorce. Minutes later, he called her cell phone, and she dissolved into tears at his angry accusations. Catching her breath, she said he was just arriving, and she couldn't face him. I excused myself and went to the parking lot. I had no description, but I knew him instantly. I had seen the same angry countenance on the man in my mirror for more than a decade.

I asked, "Hi, are you Johnny's father?"

He snarled, "Yes, who are you?"

I replied, "I'm the fire chaplain who has been with your son and his mother since the accident. You're not going into the hospital angry. This is about loving a dying child, not about your anger issues. I will not referee a battle between you and his mother. Do I make myself clear? If I haven't, you'll have to go through me to get into the hospital."

He glared, and for a moment, I thought he might punch me. Finally, he meekly surrendered and apologized. We joined hands and prayed for a miracle for his son, the little redheaded boy on life support. Later that day, I stood with both parents as they gave doctors permission to turn off life support and to harvest their son's organs. Grieving, they stood together and said good-bye to their beautiful little redheaded boy. It was another bitter cup of grief. Before the funeral, a pastor helped me put it into perspective.

He said, "Bob, if you were God, would you rather have a beautiful redheaded seven-year-old bouncing around the throne in heaven or you?" The answer was obvious. It wasn't even close. Every once in a while, I visit his gravesite just to say hi. I'll look for him in heaven, bouncing near the throne.

Walking through the fire headquarters lobby several years later, a voice called out, "Chaplain George? Chaplain Bob George. Is that you?"

I turned to see a smiling, well-dressed man approach. "Yes, but I'm sorry, do I know you?"

He replied, "We met in the parking lot ... at the hospital ... my son ... the redhead ... don't you remember?"

Embarrassed, I answered, "Yes, of course, I do. Please forgive me. How are you? You look sharp. What brings you down here?"

He said, "I've never forgotten that day and how you saved me from my anger. I'm attending a ministry school, and I'm here to interview for the fire department, and who knows, maybe one day even be a chaplain. I'd like to help others, like you helped us that day. Thank you. I'll never forget you."

In a few minutes, he was called for his interview, and after wishing him my best, we parted. I found a quiet place and thanked God, very glad that it is His work to change angry hearts, not mine. On occasion, tears still come for the little redheaded boy. Did I mention he reminded me of my grandson?

AN EMPTY BED?

The dispatch center received a call from a woman in Oregon asking for a chaplain to pray over her elderly, dying brother in a nearby trauma center. The call was directed to me. The ICU doctor advised that the patient was on life support and was dying from unknown systemic failure. He said that exhaustive tests had failed to give diagnostic clarity, and with brain activity slowing, death was imminent. With his permission, I anointed the corpse-like patient with oil and prayed for God to receive his spirit through the grace found in Jesus Christ. After leaving, I phoned his appreciative sister in Oregon and assured her that I would return the next day to update her on his condition. The second day, I returned and, walking into the ICU room, found a man sitting up in bed eating a meal. Thinking I was in the wrong room, I went to the nurses' station and asked if the patient I sought had died overnight. She smiled and replied that shortly after I left, he had spontaneously awakened, pulled his ventilator tube out, and asked for a meal. Astonished, I returned to the room and introduced myself. He said that he remembered me praying over him and then leaving the day before. The man before me appeared healthy, very different from the corpse-like patient I had anointed the day before. I called his sister and gave her the amazing news. I also said that I would check on him the following day. On the third day, finding an empty bed, I asked a nurse for his room number. She said that he had been discharged that morning, as the doctors could find no reason to keep him hospitalized. I again called his sister in Oregon and gave her the good news. She politely thanked me. I've never spoken with either again. Lord, thank you! But why him? Why not the little redheaded boy? Oh, sovereign Lord, Your ways are far beyond man's understanding.

HE DID!

The pager's harsh beeping jarred me away from my plans for the day. The dispatcher asked me to call a firefighter in need of assistance.

I did.

"My dad's dying of melanoma. He's at the hospital. Will you come?" The M word cut through me like a warm knife through butter. It's something only survivors truly understand. I told him I'd be glad to come.

After a short drive, I found the comatose man alone in a critical care room, breathing only by ventilator. The nurse said his prognosis was grim, and death was imminent. She continued that he had been unresponsive for days and hadn't spoken or eaten in over a week. Unable to block the rapid spread of disease, he was now only receiving palliative treatment for pain. She also said that his son had decided to withdraw life support.

With her permission, I approached the comatose man and quietly introduced myself without response. Opening my Bible, I read several psalms aloud. As I read Psalm 23, I thought one of his eyes fluttered but unsure continued reading until his left eye opened and focused on me. I asked him to blink twice if he could hear me.

He did.

I asked him to blink twice if he understood he was near death and would soon stand before God.

He did.

I asked him to blink twice if he knew Jesus Christ and that he was going to heaven. He stared without blinking until a solitary tear slid down his left cheek.

Taking his cold hand, I asked him to squeeze my hand if he would like to receive God's forgiveness of sins and to receive the eternal life promised through Jesus Christ.

He did.

I spoke a short prayer simply asking for God's grace and forgiveness of sins on his behalf through Jesus Christ. I asked him to squeeze my hand three times if he agreed with the prayer.

He did, almost putting me on my knees.

When I read several passages assuring him of salvation, several more tears came, and then his eye closed. Only the respirator's mechanical breathing remained.

After leaving my contact information for his son, I excused myself. He died a few minutes after the son had life support removed that afternoon. I hope to meet his dad again in heaven. I think he'll remember me.

I DO!

I have been blessed to perform marriages for several nieces and nephews, and I have also been blessed to perform several firefighters' weddings over the years. Joe and I clicked while on ride-alongs on his busy engine. One day he surprised me and asked if I would marry him and his fiancée. Throughout premarital counseling, I found them to be a good match and truly in love.

It was early June, and a hot breeze blew through the park located in the brush-covered foothills. Stiff offshore winds and low humidity for several days had brought high fire warnings to the county. While the bride and groom were taking pictures before the wedding, family and friends sought the welcome shade under the park's great oak trees. As the groomsmen mounted a fire engine brought by on-duty buddies for wedding photos, a faint odor of smoke blew into the park. Light smoke and ash soon followed, and the engine was called into service on a quickly spreading wildfire. As the engine departed with red lights and siren, the park ranger alerted the wedding party they may soon be asked to evacuate, since winds were driving the fire toward the park. Like true firefighters, his groomsmen appeared anxious to respond to the fire rather than continuing with the ceremony, but we pressed on.

I hurriedly assembled the wedding party, and with more sirens from responding units in the distance, they spoke vows before God, family, and friends. With ash raining down from the June sky, the firefighter and his beautiful bride both said, "I do!"

Shortly after the ceremony, he transferred battalions, and we lost contact. Late last year, while walking across the quad at headquarters, I heard a friendly voice. "Hey, Chaplain Bob, is that you?"

Turning, I saw Joe approaching. With smiles and hugs, we reunited after eleven years. He eagerly pulled out his phone and showed me two beautiful children, and I beamed like a proud grandfather. After a few minutes, he was called back to training, and I was off to a busy day. Driving away, I smiled and remembered the day the firefighter and his beautiful bride both said, "I do!"

It was a good day for a firefighter to get married. The day ash rained from a June sky. It just happened to be the same June day that Judy and I said, "I do!" many years before. I was blessed to have played a part in his wedding. His pictures were icing on the cake.

FIRE DISPATCHERS

The Dispatch Center is responsible for all fire, medical, and non-police 911 calls twenty-four hours a day, 365 days a year. It is an emotionally exhausting task to constantly deal with those in physical and emotional crisis. After dispatching aid on a call, they are usually on to the next emergency call and seldom know the outcome of their critical work. When I have concluded a callout, I have made it a practice to contact them, particularly when children or firefighters were involved. They have always been appreciative for the follow-up. When possible, I also drop into dispatch to "show the flag." I've never viewed myself as a morale booster, but since doing so, hugs and smiles seem to have risen, and radio voices have turned into real people. Firefighters are considered public heroes, often deservedly so, but dispatchers are quiet heroes with a tough job at the heart of the fire family.

A HERO'S DEATH

Several years ago, I was asked to assist the United States Army with a death notification. Just a few days before, a battle in Afghanistan had been reported on television news, resulting in American casualties. I met the captain and master sergeant in a parking lot near the family's residence. They thanked me for joining them, explaining that no military chaplain was available. As we prepared for the death notification, I sensed a deep caring for the soldier and family that had been absent during the Viet Nam era. During those years, tens of thousands of death notifications were sent by telegram and impersonally delivered by a cab driver. At that time, empathy was considered a disorder in the military.

As we approached the residence, a young woman stood just inside the screen door while excited voices cheered for a football game in the living room. She stared at the three uniformed strangers approaching, and before the captain could say a word, she backed away, screaming hysterically until collapsing to the hallway floor. Family members seeing us on the front walk joined the chorus of agony before a word was ever spoken. Nearby neighbors emerged staring, but seeing our uniforms, they understood and retreated back inside. My own war grief from decades before was difficult to check, and I wanted desperately to run from the screams as painful memories resurfaced. Once the initial shock dissipated, the captain spoke gracefully to the family, and I was asked to pray with them. We gathered in the living room near the official photograph of a young army ranger proudly wearing his uniform. Returning home three hours later, I was exhausted. Judy held me as I cried. A week later, the young hero's remains were returned by the government to his family's care. He was buried with full military honors, and many people lined the procession route to honor an American hero.

Though I have tried, I cannot erase his young wife's screams.

Unless they have served in the armed forces, I believe politicians should be required to accompany a military death notification before running for state or national elected office. They would better understand the honor of a soldier's service and ultimate sacrifice for America.

FROM ASHES

The wildfire had burned through the dry foothills like a speeding train consuming everything in its path. Most residents of the canyon had little time to evacuate and left with only a few precious items. I joined several fire chaplains at the evacuation center trying to calm anxious fears. The second day, with the fire moving past and operations complete in the canyon, we began escorting residents for a brief visit to the sites deemed safe by the incident commander. I cautioned the couple I escorted against the danger of flare-ups in the ashes of their home. Their hilltop house had once stood three stories with a commanding view of surrounding hills, mountains, and distant ocean. Before the fire, it was the home many dream about. Now it was a nightmare of barren ash and smoldering firebrands. Stunned, the husband stood near what had been a converted barn housing a half-dozen expensively restored automobiles. They had been reduced to pools of melted steel and aluminum. His wife and I walked slowly around the footprint of their home. She sobbed quietly at the sight of melted appliances and melted dreams while gusting canyon winds blew wisps of smoke and ash into the air. I stood quietly, allowing them time to grieve their loss.

She asked me to find a prized photo album she had mistakenly left by the door in their hurried evacuation. I carefully stepped into the hot ashes where the front door once welcomed friends and family, but the destruction appeared complete. Turning, I stepped on a small, hard object buried in ash and recovered a broken Hummel figurine with a date on it. She immediately recognized it as a treasured birthday gift to her daughter. Holding the warm figurine to her heart, she tearfully related how she had given one to her daughter on each birthday until she turned twenty-one. She had stored them in a box in the attic awaiting her daughter's graduation from college. Carefully, I stepped back into the ashes and found a second, and a third, and another until twenty unbroken figurines were recovered. They had fallen three stories from the attic in the midst of a raging fire and survived. They were the only items found intact from the ashes where a house once stood, but they meant everything to a heartbroken woman. Her thank you hug and tears told me so.

TEMPUS FUGIT

I remember only one phrase from my ninth grade Latin class, "tempus fugit," meaning "time flies." It certainly does. Now in my seventieth year, I watch as hours turn into days, which fly into weeks, which blur into … well, you get it. Our oldest granddaughter had just begun her plebe year as a "midi" at the Naval Academy and her brother his freshman year at

Chico State University, when I was challenged to write this book. Today we have just returned from their graduations and her commissioning as a naval ensign. Four years have passed like the wind, and my body and mind are telling me to hurry with the book. Time is erasing many memories both good and bad. It has an unwavering way of doing that to everyone. I write hoping both Sandra and Michael will better know the man who married their mother and entered their lives without a vote. I also desire my grandchildren to better know the character of the man they sometimes call "Grumps," and how he became the grandfather they know, warts and all. Most of all, I want them, or anyone reading this book, to understand that if they see anything worthwhile, anything of value, anything to be admired in my life, it is due solely to the grace of the Lord Jesus Christ. My story began as a selfish, naïve kid who walked away from God, lost his dreams, his honor, and almost himself. Thankfully my story didn't end there, but it continues even today with God's redemptive calling to be a godly man and fire chaplain. By His grace, I hope to end my journey well, so I will strive for obedience until I hear His persistent voice say, "Well done good and faithful servant; you were faithful with a few things, I will put you in charge of many things. Come and share your Master's happiness" (Matthew 25:21, NIV).

Until that day, I will continue the journey I am on with thanksgiving. By His grace, I will continue to answer the call to assist those in need, and I will never forget the words inscribed on a thousand dog tags, "I will be strong and courageous. I will not be terrified or discouraged; for the Lord my God is with me wherever I go" (Joshua 1:9 paraphrased).

POSTSCRIPT

The journey has been amazing, the pain at times unbearable, the failures epic, and the successes God's. I never intended to write about myself but have been encouraged by the prayers and cheerleading of my wife, close friends, Katie, Dale, John, and a stranger. He crossed my path in a hotel lobby in Annapolis on Parent's Day weekend in 2012. During a brief conversation, he asked a few questions, listened intently to my responses, and gave me an exhortation to "write your story." His words burned in my heart. At first, I blinked in fear and procrastinated. *What if I write a book, and no one cares? Why is my story any more important than anyone else's?* Such questions no longer matter, but obedience does. I pray that some will learn from my failures and choose to walk with God far sooner than I did. Indeed many pages in this book were written with tears as painful memories and failures were relived. Perhaps if I had applied The Citadel's simple plebe answers more readily in life, I could have avoided the painfully foolish years spent running from God, making bad choices while looking to blame others. Through the journey, I have learned that honor is more than a learned code of behavior. It is a renewed heart and a life of faith in Christ as His words declare, "Whoever serves me must follow me; and where I am, my servant also will be. My Father will honor the one who serves me" (John 12:26, NIV). By following and serving Jesus Christ, I have found honor that no man can take away.

"Yes, sir. No, sir. No excuse, sir!"

My sword I give to him that shall succeed me in my pilgrimage, and my courage and skill to him that can get it. My works and scars I carry with me, to be a witness for me that I have fought His battles who now shall be my rewarder. So he passed over and all the trumpets sounded for him—on the other side.

—*Pilgrims' Progress*

Tempus Fugit

CPSIA information can be obtained
at www.ICGtesting.com
Printed in the USA
FSOW02n1511310117
30234FS

9 781512 761979